Museums Without Barriers

A new deal for disabled people

Fondation de France/ICOM

FONDATION
DE
FRANCE

ICOM

in conjunction with Routledge
London and New York

First published 1991
by Routledge
11 New Fetter Lane, London EC4P 4EE

Simultaneously published in the USA and Canada
by Routledge
a division of Routledge, Chapman and Hall, Inc.
29 West 35th Street, New York, NY 10001

© 1991 Fondation de France/ICOM

English translations: Margaret Rubens

Printed in Great Britain by Butler & Tanner Ltd,
Frome and London

British Library Cataloguing in Publication Data applied for
Library of Congress Cataloging in Publication Data applied for
ISBN 0–415–05454–0
    0–415–06994–7 (pbk)

Printed on permanent paper in accordance with the American NISO Standard

Contents

Contents

Contents

Contents

List of illustrations

Figures

Plates
between pages 80 and 81

List of illustrations

Foreword

On 7 and 8 November 1988 a European conference on 'Museums and the Disabled' was held at UNESCO House in Paris. Organized by the Fondation de France, in collaboration with various other bodies, this conference brought together experts from all over Europe and presented some remarkable achievements, both from France and abroad.

This book is a collection of the conference speakers' papers which are rounded out with the experiences and reflections of other experts in the field, both on the different types of handicap as well as on possible ways of making museums accessible to all.

In preparing this book we have tried, within the measure of our means, to break down a few of the barriers that keep human beings apart and, at the same time, to respect the identity of each and every individual.

We take this occasion to express our deepest gratitude to the Fondation Otis, which supported both the conference and the publication of this book.

Bernard Latarjet
Director-General of the Fondation de France

Preface

It is satisfying to note that parallel to the overwhelming interest shown in museums today, these same institutions are anxious to meet the demands of those of us who, either temporarily or permanently, suffer from some form of disablement.

For very many years, the International Council of Museums (ICOM) has promoted the opening-up of museums to an ever wider public and the development of close links with every section of the community. It has encouraged them to play a decisive role in non-formal education, and to fulfil not only the cultural but also the social function which is expected of them nowadays by all those working in the field of culture and development. It has given wide recognition to initiatives taken in favour of the disabled and has recommended, notably during the ICOM Eleventh General Conference in 1977, that museums take active steps to ensure maximum accessibility and to expand adequately adapted programmes.

I should like to pay tribute here to all those who, throughout the world, are striving to make the museum a place which is truly accessible to everyone. They all work in close co-operation with associations and institutions and benefit from the latters' advice and support.

In 1988, greatly to its credit, the Fondation de France brought together speakers from a wide variety of backgrounds to discuss the subject 'Museums and Disabled People'. The conference was highly successful and I very much hope that this publication, which is both a record and an extension of those discussions, will be a source of inspiration for new initiatives all over the world.

Alpha Oumar Konaré
President of ICOM

I

Cultural policies concerning disabled people, in France and abroad

European policy for the integration of disabled people into cultural life

Bernhard M. Wehrens

The Commission of European Communities, and more specifically the Division for Actions in Favour of Disabled People, have always sought to achieve optimum self-fulfilment for the disabled and development of all the talents they possess. A major aim of the Community is thus to increase the degree of independence enjoyed by these people, in the cultural field as elsewhere, of course.

I would therefore like briefly to present a few of the general ideas behind what the European Communities are doing with this in view.

In its Resolution dated 27 June 1974 instituting the first Community programme of action for the professional rehabilitation of the disabled, the Council of Ministers lays stress on the general purpose of the Community's efforts on behalf of all disabled persons, which must be to provide the necessary assistance to permit them to lead a normal life as perfectly assimilated members of society with regular access to cultural activities. A vital prerequisite will naturally be elimination of the architectural obstacles to their mobility, and the Commission therefore subsequently brought together a group of experts. This group drew up a list of minimum requirements in connection with access for users of wheelchairs to such public buildings as theatres, cinemas and museums, for example, and with itineraries for these visitors inside the buildings.

They began by emphasizing that, while the percentage of physically handicapped people within the population of any given country was higher than generally supposed, the measures to be adopted must not be determined by considerations of number. Most of us may at various stages in our lives – in old age, in pregnancy, or after an accident – suffer if only temporary disablement, and the general concern must be with enabling any citizen who happens to find him- or herself in such a situation to live as normal a life as possible. There is one encouraging thing: we find people tending more and more distinctly to adjust their surroundings to the changes in their way of living; the human imagination is fertile in this respect and suitable alterations in public buildings may provide a solution to the problems specific to the mentally and/or physically handicapped. But it must be confessed that the present situation is still a very long way from what is implied in the achievement of this ideal and it is therefore vitally necessary to enforce strong and immediate action for compliance with minimum standards of accessibility if we are to avoid the disaster which would result from the annual building of hundreds of public buildings inaccessible to the disabled, and especially to users of wheelchairs.

According to the experts the adapting of buildings to suit the specific requirements of the disabled will turn out to be beneficial to the community as a whole. Our long-term goal must therefore be newly designed surroundings into which all disabled people, including users of wheelchairs, can fit without needing any special assistance. The experts recommended minimum standards of two kinds, as described below.

The 'Type 2' standards, recommended first of all, are designed to serve the needs of disabled persons including users of ordinary wheelchairs and thus involve the provision, in museums, theatres and cinemas, of sufficient space for them to move about, and of the appropriate installations. According to the experts, adoption of the provisions of these standards (for example, easy to turn taps, non-skid floorings, windows low enough for a seated person to see out of them without difficulty, absence of raised thresholds indoors, etc.) would permit disabled people to lead as independent a life as their disability allowed.

The 'Type 1' standards, designed to permit minimum accessibility, should be made compulsory in all new building work. They would serve to further the objective of social and cultural integration by enabling disabled people to visit what are described as 'cultural' institutions.

The experts are, however, conscious of the fact that the practical adoption of these standards within the framework of the current national legislation is liable to raise problems. For this reason the Commission intends to call a meeting of government-appointed experts to examine the ways and means of enforcing standards as early as possible under a draft directive governing the transport of persons with a walking handicap.

For the pilot-research projects the Council of Ministers drew up a list of priorities on which absolute pride of place was given to social and professional integration. It was felt essential to eliminate architectural obstacles to the movement of disabled people both indoors and out of doors. Three pieces of applied research were thus proposed, namely:

1. An assessment of the technical difficulties and costs involved in the adaptation of dwellings to suit the needs of the disabled in an urban context.
2. An assessment of the effect of such alterations on the success or otherwise of the rehabilitation measures adopted for the occupiers.
3. An assessment of the technical features of the alterations involved.

In all three cases the findings were of great assistance to the Council for the evaluation of the Commission's recommendations in the matter.

The research was carried out simultaneously in eight member states: Denmark, France, the Federal Republic of Germany, Luxembourg, the Netherlands, the United Kingdom, Ireland and Italy. In Ireland a report was recently drawn up by the Arts Council on the possibilities of access for disabled people to theatres, cinemas, art galleries, etc. The Arts Council report based itself on the fact that places of entertainment, art exhibitions, etc. must first of all be reached, and that transport will therefore be necessary. It thus adopted the code 'TO ENABLE', composed of T = transport, O = outside, E = entrance and exit, N = notifications, A = areas of venue, B = bars and restaurants, L = loos/lavatories, E = extras (catalogues, interpreters, etc.). The Abbey and Peacock theatres in Dublin have already adopted this system.

Another pilot project I would mention is the one in France at Evry, subsidized by the Commission. The architect for this was Mr Louis-Pierre Grosbois, who is one of the contributors to this collection.

In view of all these projects and existing situations, the Commission is essentially out to tackle the problem of the accessibility of buildings used for cultural purposes, with the aim of total integration of able-bodied and disabled alike. To achieve this end it appeals to all organizations, whether public or private, which cater for disabled persons to join forces with a view to co-operation on a European scale.

Creativity has become an increasingly important feature of the lives of disabled people. This is the reason for the founding, under the impetus of the Commission, of EUROCREA (European Association for the Creativity of the Disabled) with a Board composed so that each member state of the Community has on it at least one representative. Within this framework, there are to be several specific kinds of activity.

On the national level the main role of the national committees (set up and given impetus by the national representative on the Board) will consist in providing liaison between the national and the European activities and in arranging for information concerning Europe as a whole to reach those concerned within their respective countries.

At the European level the task of the Association is to stimulate the activities of the national committees and co-ordinate any European initiatives. Among the annual activities envisaged I will mention in particular the organizing of three-day plenary European seminars with an attendance of around three hundred, the holding of national seminars, the making of grants to disabled persons who are to take advanced courses and the creation of a documentation and information centre specific to the area concerned.

It will therefore be readily understood that in order to defend these various ideas and projects medium-term objectives must be met which call for genuine co-operation on a European scale.

The policy of the Ministry of Culture in France

Dominique Charvet

I would like to thank the Fondation de France, which has had no small share in the initiative of holding this symposium, and which has given us the opportunity of stating the policies of the various cultural authorities with regard to disabled people as they presently stand. And on my own behalf I would like to say that the Ministry of Culture very naturally has a policy marked by a certain number of initiatives and experiments which I shall be coming to a little later on, but which will be mainly dealt with by subsequent contributors specially competent in each of the different cultural sectors. Before going on to these I feel it is my duty as speaker for the Ministry to try to suggest some of the possible approaches for a theoretical examination of the problem of the specific action to be taken by a Ministry of Culture on the questions at issue here. Whatever the practical efforts achieved by any given institution – and, as you will see, they are many in number – it is, I feel, legitimate to seek to ascertain whether that institution is taking the steps which will make its achievement at once necessary and irreplaceable. In view of what physical and mental handicaps mean I feel that the authorities in charge of culture cannot but pay them particular attention and take a strong stand in the matter.

To concern oneself with culture is, I feel, to concern oneself with the perceptible universe, or, to be more concrete still, with the senses. Nothing is more touching than the spectacle of a Beethoven grown deaf, or a Degas with declining sight. It is a part of the ultimate aim of culture to give us access to greater understanding and to stronger sensation, to illuminate our vision and sharpen our hearing. Hence those whose business is with culture cannot but be more deeply touched and concerned than others by whatever cuts men and women off from a certain number of objects of perception. The encounter with creation itself makes us feel how blind we are to the light we personally would have been powerless to paint, or how deaf to melodies we would have been unable to sing or play. Creation brings us face to face with our own shortcomings and with the relative incapacity of our senses and imagination. The creator who reveals other images or other sounds to the ordinary able-bodied person is doing for that person precisely what is done for disabled people by those who strive to give them access to the sensations common to the rest of us.

Culture is also a set of values which provide the foundation for a life in common – which distinguish the beautiful from the ugly, the normal from the abnormal or the good from the bad. We know very well that our fundamental attitude to a handicap will ultimately be based on a judgement, explicit or otherwise, on beauty and ugliness and also on the normal as distinct from the abnormal, and even – for what is there to prevent it? – on good as distinct from bad. The gaze that turns aside from a face or from a view of suffering, or the ears which refuse to hear too peculiar a sound, are themselves the reflection of an upbringing and of a culture specific to a given people at a given period. Too often there will be deliberate rejection over and above the sense of being different.

The handicap consists in being unable to 'do' something, and this again is a challenge to the imperative to create which stimulates the artist. When some great painter is said to have his brushes fixed to his fingertips because he can no longer hold them, he shows us the road to resistance and to refusal to be confined within the limits of our handicap.

I feel therefore that, if we have a cultural policy in the matter today, it must provide for three main courses of action. At the outset, we must adopt a clear line of non-differentiation and non-discrimination. At first sight this would appear to be the regular duty of the welfare administrations. However, for the reasons I have given, my Ministry has, I feel, the very special duty of combating the judgements – not to say the bogeys – connected with the world of the disabled. Just as it has acted with determination in the combating of their exclusion from society, it can have a specific and privileged role in the promotion of the programmes which must be launched jointly.

In the second place, there must of course be removal of all the obstacles preventing access to the heritage for which my Ministry is responsible. For this purpose, a great deal has been done in the way of alterations to the big theatres such as the Comédie-Française, the Palais de Chaillot and the Odéon, and also to the big Paris museums. This work of adapting cultural premises must be pursued, on the basis of the examples set by such outstanding achievements as the Musée d'Orsay, where the signposting and the system of itineraries for visitors are particularly remarkable. But I feel that not merely the premises but the works themselves must be made more accessible. Here I may mention a number of initiatives which in my opinion are likewise examples to be followed: the Direction du Livre et de la Lecture supports the running of a lending library in Grenoble, the work of the National Agency for Technical Aids and Special Printing for the Visually Handicapped and also the Academy of Sign Language and the Centre for Transcription and Publication in Braille in Toulouse. Similarly the Direction de la Musique et de la Danse is supporting a scheme for the designing of a hearing aid for deaf children, and also a scheme launched by an association known as 'Sémaphore' for the adapting of musical instruments for use by the handicapped. The Direction des Archives de France has fitted its public reading rooms with booths in which the people who accompany the non-sighted can read out documents and record their contents for use by the latter, while the Direction des Musées de France has taken a certain number of initiatives of its own for the non-sighted, notably at the Musée de Cluny, the Museum of African and Oceanic Arts and the Louvre; the Cluny experiment has been filmed.

There is also a third form of practical initiative. I would say it was a primary necessity for the disabled to be able to do creative work themselves. I believe I am stating a self-evident truth: do disabled people not represent those among us who are most familiar with the imperative of creating, or re-creating, their senses and their lives?

Access to historical monuments for disabled people: the policy of the Direction du Patrimoine (French Directorate of the Heritage)

Anne Magnant

The term 'historical monument' has in practice a great variety of meanings. There are 36,000 historical monuments in France, some private and others public, some open to visitors and others in re-use for one or other of a number of purposes: frequently they house cultural bodies, but they may also provide premises for administrative departments or public welfare services. Others are not open to the public at all; the majority of these are places of worship, owned by the municipal authorities.

The responsibility of the state as regards readier access for the disabled to historical monuments is generally confined to the adaptation of the buildings. But the state also has a special responsibility for those historical monuments it owns which are open to visitors. And besides making these physically and materially more accessible the state can also encourage whatever is done to facilitate the admission of disabled persons.

Accessibility of historical monuments: a difficult problem

Buildings are protected as historical monuments either by listing or by inclusion in the Supplementary Inventory of Historical Monuments. In the former case the interest they present from the point of view of architecture or history must, the law says, be of a 'public' nature, while in the latter it need merely be 'sufficient'.

By definition, historical monuments may be located in an infinite variety of places, and their architecture and structure may be of widely varying kinds. They are architectural legacies of history. The very reasons which warrant their protection require that they be preserved in the form in which history has handed them down; their very character makes it extremely difficult to introduce facilities for the specific benefit of the disabled visitor, owing to their intrinsic nature or architecture or to archaeological or aesthetic factors.

Cultur-

There are places where the nature of the location practically precl
one from envisaging any such special facilities: for example, the Mo·
Michel perched on its rock, the decorated underground caves in the v
of the Vézère or the Château-Gaillard with its surrounding fortifications.
Other historic buildings, on the contrary, are directly accessible. Some,
such as the Ecole de Lods in Suresnes or the many listed historic hospital
buildings, were initially designed to receive people with handicaps, while
others, such as the Epierre Abbey at Cerdon (Ain), are actually to be
turned into centres for the disabled.

Certain over-hasty schemes for alterations involving, for example, the
building of a handrail or the introduction of a lift, are unacceptable
because they would disfigure the building. In each individual case a
minutely detailed study must be made, with imagination, intelligence and
sensibility, to enable an arrangement compatible with the nature of the
particular building.

Numerous and sometimes exemplary solutions notwithstanding

Some of the many successes

In the historic buildings open to the public we find many cases of
attempted solutions to the access problem. In certain places of worship
it has been possible to introduce a sloping means of access, as at Chartres,
where a movable ramp has been fitted; where the creation of a slope is
impossible or would be scarcely acceptable for aesthetic reasons, doors
have been planned at ground level.

As a general rule, historical monuments which are readapted for public
use are subject to the provisions of common law; this applies both to
buildings re-used for a new purpose – e.g. for the housing of a town hall,
a museum or a library – and to the provision of improved facilities in
historic buildings already open to the public. Thus ramps were introduced
when the Hôtel Salé in the Marais district in Paris was adapted by the
architect Simounet in order to house the Musée Picasso. Readily accessible
lifts have also been built in the Château de Fontainebleau, south of Paris.
The Cairn of Barnenez, a group of megalithic tombs near Plouezec'h, in
Brittany, whose site has just been renovated for the benefit of visitors,
has been provided with a ramp and with toilet accommodation accessible
to the disabled. At the privately owned Château de la Roche-Corbon
(Charente-Maritime), special indoor itineraries with no steps up or down
have been provided for the disabled and a slope has been built in the
gardens to facilitate their access.

In the former priory at Salagon (Alpes-de-Haute-Provence), which now houses the Conservatoire Ethnologique de la Haute Provence, the authorities and the Alpes de Lumière association have together had a special entrance made for the disabled, and it is planned to build a ramp to enable the twelfth-century church to be more comfortably visited.

Sometimes special facilities have been devised in order to provide easier access to grounds and buildings. A little railway has long existed at Chenonceaux (Indre-et-Loire), and there is one at the privately owned Mortemer Abbey, near Ecouis (Eure). A similar one has recently been built at Versailles to take visitors on a tour of the park.

An exemplary operation

An exemplary job has recently been carried out at Aigues-Mortes (Gard), to enable people with a walking handicap to visit the ramparts. Access in general had become difficult owing to the constant increase of the number of visitors, and progress along the ramparts was hampered because of bottlenecks forming in the spiral staircases. The Direction du Patrimoine and the Caisse Nationale des Monuments Historiques (National Historical Monuments Fund), which is responsible for the admission of visitors to historic buildings owned by the state, therefore decided to make Aigues-Mortes the object of a pilot study whose purpose was to permit the admission of all the public, including the elderly and the disabled. Thus, once approval of the Higher Commission on Historical Monuments had been obtained, a lift was built inside the famous Tour de Constance and hoists, handrails and footbridges were added to enable wheelchair visitors to reach the ramparts. These visitors may now have access to all four levels of the Tour de Constance and make an 805-metre tour of the ramparts under comfortable conditions, and in 1990 they will be able to visit the museum. These improvements, which are the work of Jean-Pierre Dufoix, a senior architect and Inspector-General of the Historical Monuments Administration, were designed and tested with the aid of the local associations of disabled persons, which I believe have greatly appreciated the operation, completed about a year ago, and costing five million francs in all. I should point out, however, that the alterations were hotly criticized locally and that the Ministry of Culture was obliged to provide a whole series of explanations and particulars. A file of data is available on the whole subject.

Arrangements for receiving disabled people in historic buildings

In addition to the problem of the alterations needed in order to give disabled people physical access to historic buildings we are faced with that of the way they are received and looked after in the places less readily accessible.

In state-owned historic buildings the attendants are officially responsible for the reception of the public. They are at the service of disabled persons and quite naturally help them to overcome any obstacles. But there is no service specifically designed to meet the needs of the disabled in these buildings and the point deserves thinking about.

Certain of the associations for the preservation of the heritage are doing a remarkable job in connection with improved services of the kind required. The Club du Vieux Manoir and the Chantier Histoire et Architecture Médiévales organize tours of the buildings in their care at the request of such associations as Le Nid or Les Papillons Blancs. According to what is required in each particular case, such guided visits are either the same as those arranged for other visitors or specially adapted to suit given types of handicap.

But the activity most deserving of interest engaged by these associations consists in their arrangements for disabled young people to join the teams of volunteers working on the restoration of historical monuments. Here I would mention the Association du Vieux Chatel, at Chatel-sur-Moselle (Vosges), which, in co-operation with the official welfare authorities and the educational staff of an institution for handicapped young people, has carefully chosen areas on its huge restoration site where these young people can come and work with their teachers. This practice, which calls for no special equipment, brings the pupils from the institution into contact with other volunteer workers on the site.

The Club du Vieux Manoir seeks actually to fit disabled young people into the normal routine of restoration work. Thus once a year a group of young people with walking handicaps is received at the Château de Guise, in northern France (Aisne), where it does bricklaying and makes door-frames. Further, every two years a group of young people from a psychiatric hospital takes part, under medical supervision, in the clearing-away of rubble on the restoration site at the Abbaye des Prémontrés (Aisne). At the Castle of Argy (Indre), young people from an institution for the handicapped have, at the latter's request, joined the teams working on the restoration of the grounds.

Cultural policies concerning disabled people

The association known as Chantier Histoire et Architecture Médiévales is co-operating regularly with a psychiatric hospital in its work on the restoration site at Pouancé (Maine-et-Loire) and the young patients work under medical supervision on bricklaying and repointing. Disabled young people are also taken on at Yèvre-le-Châtel (Loiret) and Pontivy (Morbihan), and similar arrangements are made by the youth services of the Christian Movement for Peace and by the Alpes de Lumière association.

Such initiatives are encouraged by the state, which follows with the greatest of interest the work being done by these associations and annually provides financial aid for the running of the voluntary youth restoration schemes and for the training of their personnel.

Conclusion

An assessment of what has been achieved in connection with historical monuments will show far from negligible results, and significant work is being done or is on schedule where it has not actually been completed. But it is certainly possible to do more.

I feel that for this purpose there should be set up a working group of representatives from the Fondation de France, the Direction du Patrimoine and other bodies active in the historical monuments field and associations of disabled people, and that its task should be to look into the possibilities for future initiatives under the heading both of improved material facilities and of reception services.

One result of this symposium for the Direction du Patrimoine could be the formation of such a group.

'Cry Freedom' after Attenborough: a review of the work of the United Kingdom Committee of Inquiry into the Arts and Disabled People

Peter Senior

Cry Freedom is the title of Richard Attenborough's film about apartheid in South Africa. To use the title for this talk is a slight breach of copyright but I doubt whether Sir Richard would object. When he was Chairman of the Committee of Inquiry into the Arts and Disabled People (*The Attenborough Report* 1985) in Britain, he and the members were concerned about the freedom of people with disabilities to participate more fully in the arts and crafts.

In the preface to the report, Richard Attenborough said:

> The ultimate target must be to enable and encourage disabled people to play the fullest possible part in the artistic life of the community... It lies within the power of our generation to transform their lives and to enrich the world of art itself by their greater involvement. Failure to act diminishes us all.

These are stirring words. What has happened in practice?

The subsequent Carnegie Council Review (*After Attenborough: Arts and Disabled People* 1988) emphasizes the need for all – government, corporate, voluntary and public sectors – to work towards this end. The work of the Inquiry and Council is a result of an initiative by the Carnegie United Kingdom Trust, a philanthropic grant-giving body, one of the Carnegie family of institutions in Britain and the United States of America.

The latter country has seen more progress through legislation about access than witnessed in Britain and Europe, where there is no similar legislation, especially for arts venues. In Britain, there is now legislation to require proper access to new shops and offices, new single-storey employment, education centres and public buildings, and to the ground floor of multi-storey buildings. However, you will see that this does not include the thousands of older buildings which are often used for arts activities. Physical obstacles abound in older buildings, in museums and galleries, libraries, concert halls, cinemas and theatres, not to mention church and civic halls in which the arts take place.

Equally, attitudes are just as important. Staff generally have to deal with the majority and do not understand the needs of a minority, although there are good exceptions to this pessimistic view where managers are enlightened. Disability awareness training is therefore important and humanizing for staff in performance venues and in arts agencies.

Our review shows that:

1. The four national Arts Councils and some Regional Arts Associations, some health authorities and a few local authority councils have adopted a 'Code of Practice', guidelines to ensure attention to the needs of people with disabilities.
2. Some of these agencies have agreed to appoint *designated* officers to provide a responsive and responsible focal point to ensure proper attention and training.
3. There is an increase in training opportunities for students with disabilities, but these are pitiful in number compared with the need. Until disabled people can receive professional training, they are denied the chance of suitable jobs.
4. There is an increase in arts agencies wishing to include disabled people as artists and as participants in arts workshops.

There are signs in the media of an increase in knowledge and understanding of how disabled people have artistic ability, but perhaps less understanding of how more disabled people need to be in positions of responsibility to manage resources.

It is slow progress, but in two areas there are especially welcome signs. First, in the museums sector in Britain the major national organization, the Museums and Galleries Commission, is creating a post of Disabilities Officer to encourage museums nationwide to think of their responsibilities to disabled people and to respond through their subsequent needs and staff training.

Several staffs have formed MAGDA, the Museums and Galleries Disabilities Association, as a voluntary group to challenge museums and their staff by advocacy. Its Chairman, James Ford-Smith, is a Public Relations Officer with the Ulster Museum and is blind. The Secretary is Anne Pearson who is one of the contributors to this collection and who has done so much to encourage the development of touch exhibitions.

Her book *Arts for Everyone* and her work as Administrator for the Carnegie Council have added substantially to progress.

Education officers attached to individual museums are initiating better access to displays and are developing touch exhibitions to benefit many, not only the visually handicapped.

Second, in the health care sector of hospitals, hospices and clinics, where every patient may be considered to be at least temporarily disabled, we are witnessing a better understanding of the purpose and role of the arts. There are increasing numbers of artists, designers, craftspeople, musicians, theatre groups, puppeteers, poets, for example, being commissioned to work in places of health care, and on a wide variety of interesting projects. The local health authorities and the government's Department of Health are much more aware of the existence and need for these arts programmes. It has, however, to be continually stressed that this work is complementary to the work of the various professional arts therapists who largely work in the hospitals. There are an encouraging number of schemes which involve taking patients or former patients to arts venues such as museums and galleries, theatres and concert halls.

Slowly but surely, the social services are beginning to recognize the valuable part that arts activities can play in community care. For the elderly, 'Reminiscence Therapy' has been seen as a very appropriate activity providing many opportunities for valuable links with local museums and galleries.

The new 'Arts for Health' centre in Manchester (when it gains adequate funding as I'm sure it will) will provide an information and consultancy focus for development of new schemes and standards throughout the United Kingdom. A primary role of the centre is to work closely with health care authorities and hospital managers to advise on better provision of arts services.

There is a great deal of interest by architects in planning for the arts in new hospitals and other health buildings, and this is encouraged by the government's Department of Health. An active campaign is under way by the Arts Council of Great Britain to press government and local authorities to adopt a scheme for one per cent of all new building costs to be allocated to the provision of art in that building. This would make a huge difference, as it has in other countries.

The *Attenborough Report* and Carnegie Council Review *After Attenborough* were primarily about the needs of the individual and how to ensure adequate integration in facilities and activities. There is a new movement in Britain, for a 'disability arts culture' and while this is fine for those who want and need such a separate culture, there are many artists and others with a disability who are very certain that they wish to be known for their talent and art and not for their disability. 'Artability', not disability. 'Disabled art' for them is not an option.

That is mainly why we support any initiatives and the creation of any resources to ensure integrated activity where possible and not segregated activity unless absolutely necessary. We want able-bodied and less able-bodied people to learn from each other. It is, of course, important that more disabled people are involved in the management of resources to ensure that they are an effective voice in future policy-making.

We look for positive thinking in action – not negative attitudes such as those unfortunately being exhibited at present by the Conservative government towards the idea of a special 'Adaptations Fund' which would award challenge grants to arts venues which desire to make improvements in all forms of access. Important needs cover ramps, lifts, car parking, loop-hearing systems for the hard of hearing, telephones at correct height, computers for information, signs at venues and good publicity; not only for audience participation but for employment. These are equally important in museums and galleries and in other arts venues.

I hope that this brief summary encapsulates some of the main points from our reports. Both the *Attenborough Report* and the Carnegie Council Review *After Attenborough* are worth reading because the position in France must be very similar to that in Britain. We wish you success with your work and progress.

Facilities for disabled people in French national museums

Alain Erlande-Brandenburg

As a museum curator I have no need to tell you – and I shall be addressing you as a practitioner – how essential it is from the point of view of professional ethics for the entire population to be made welcome in our museum institutions, all together and at the same time, with no exceptions. I emphasize this point particularly because I feel it is a vital factor in all the exploration forming the natural prelude to the necessary action to be taken in the matter. There must be no special hours, no areas reserved for given persons: provision must be made – and this obviously will mean difficulties – for all visitors to be able to meet together and run into each other in front of the works we exhibit.

One of the main difficulties, especially in France and in some of the Mediterranean countries, is that museum institutions are housed in historical monuments and that for this very reason the difficulties which exist in the case of buildings coming under the Direction du Patrimoine are to be met with again in our museums; such buildings are difficult to adapt, especially where the museums are old ones.

Everything is naturally different when we embark on a new operation. We shall be coming later on to the case of the Musée d'Orsay, which, I believe, is quite a spectacular success, and also to that of the Greater Louvre, where you will see that the study made of the whole scheme as a prelude to the action taken was absolutely exemplary. The same sort of problem arose in the case of the Musée Picasso in Paris, housed in a splendid mid-eighteenth-century building; but this was a new operation and it was therefore possible to try to resolve the difficulty at the outset. I would say this was the easiest sort of case, in so far as, of course – and I believe this is always the big problem – one does not come up against psychological difficulties when dealing with either the architect or the curator.

Where museums are already housed in existing historic buildings the operation is generally far more difficult and sometimes even impossible. Here I would like to take two examples, one in which it was feasible and the other where I gave up the attempt. I say 'I' merely because I personally dealt with both cases. The museums were the Musée de Cluny and the Musée d'Ecouen.

The Musée de Cluny is housed in two buildings, one dating from the fifteenth and the other from the third century, on the slopes of the Montagne Sainte Geneviève, and the difference in level between them is so great that it could not be hoped to remedy things by building a balustrade. Obviously an attempt must be made to solve the problem of Cluny, and I will venture to hope that this will be done some day, since there is a scheme for turning the place as a whole into the big Museum of the Middle Ages which we at present lack; perhaps it will be possible in the process to find an answer to the tricky questions arising out of abrupt changes in ground level.

Things were quite different at Ecouen. Not that the operation had not already been launched when I took up the basic question of the admission of the physically disabled; but it was possible to resolve it, to start with because of the visible will to do so on the part both of the architect and of the museological specialists in charge. A further reason was that the sixteenth-century design of the building provided for three storeys and that the changes in level turned out to be slight enough to be readily dealt with. The main difficulty was that of access from one floor to another, and admittedly here a definite choice had to be made; perhaps it ran contrary to the wishes of the curator, since I abandoned the idea of having the lift go right up to the fourth level so as to enable it to be large enough, and this meant it could not reach the attic floor where the reserve collections were kept. Once again, this was a decision involving a difficulty for the curator, who is thus unable to move material from the attics except by hand; but it provided an entirely satisfactory solution to the problem of access for the disabled to the ground floor and first and second floors. Today the Musée d'Ecouen is accessible to all the physically disabled. So much for my first point.

I would now like to deal with a second point which I feel to be just as important – or perhaps more so in that it ties up with the previous one: I am referring to the access that the visually handicapped and the blind should be able to have to works of art. Here again I will speak from my own experience, according to which knowledge of an object is based equally on visual analysis and on touch. To touch and feel an object is, for the curator, quite as important as to see it. This is obviously not as true of paintings, where the visual contact will suffice, as of anything that possesses volume, whether sculpture, objects made from textiles, or metal, for example.

The three techniques involved here all call for a tactile approach in addition to a visual one. We have come to the conclusion that in the case of the visually handicapped the tactile approach should be rendered more effective through the placing in their hands of authentic objects, and I would like to lay emphasis on this point, which I feel to be fundamental. It is true that a cast of a medieval piece of sculpture will suffice for an understanding of both volume and form, but it will fail to provide what I consider as essential, namely, the material itself, which, if it is not always a decisive factor as regards the form given to the work, nevertheless has unquestionably an influence. A sculptor obviously does not set about carving a hard limestone, a marble and a softer stone all in the same way, and it is essential for the visually handicapped to become aware of this. Similarly, you can sense all the difference there is between the feel of a marble and the feel of a particularly warm stone. I am therefore of the opinion that it is vitally necessary to make such original objects as are unlikely to suffer harm from touching available to the non-sighted; and if the reserve collections of museums are sometimes something of a myth they nevertheless contain objects which may readily be handled but which are not for all that second-class exhibits.

I would specially emphasize this in the case of sculpture, since it is possible to identify carving that has been done with a stonecutter's chisel, at least if the fingers have been taught the right degree of sensitivity; it is present in the fingers of the curator and I see no reason why those of the visually handicapped should not possess it too. It is at all events one of our important tasks to see that they do.

Let us take another equally important material, stained glass. Touch alone can distinguish an original window from a nineteenth-century copy, and my friend the art historian Grodecki, whose sight had grown very poor with age, always felt a stained-glass window instead of looking at it; he was able to distinguish a twelfth-century work from a clumsy copy dating from the last century by exploring the very fine layer of *grisaille* used to outline the forms and draw in the clothes and the folds in the clothing.

The same sort of distinction may be made with tapestry: a tapestry is made of threads, but not just any threads, and the sensation obtained through touch readily enables wool to be distinguished from silk and silk from metal threads. Here again, these are factors vital to an understanding of the work and of the role of the materials in the work as a whole.

Cultural policies concerning disabled people

I will come lastly to metals. Metals may be seen, touched and smelt. Perhaps you will have noticed this among the great historians and the great specialists in gold and silver ware of your acquaintance: they judge silver by its smell; the differences in smell enable the different periods of manufacture to be distinguished.

This general approach – which, once again, is not suitable in the case of paintings – must be the one we choose: we must take steps to make original exhibits directly available to as large a public as possible, so that the visually handicapped, the non-sighted and the ordinary visitor may understand the part played by the medium in a work of art. This is certainly not enough, but it is one aspect of perception.

My last point relates to architecture: how are we to give a visually handicapped or non-sighted person an understanding of what Chartres Cathedral signifies, and how are we to enable such people to conceive of the spatial reality of Bourges, which is its antithesis, though built at the same period? This is obviously a very subtle task, and we are obliged to use models, in other words reproductions in miniature, of these huge buildings. Here again, I feel an enormous amount of thinking needs to be done on the subject of how the historic buildings visited by the visually handicapped may be rendered relatively understandable; it is a task to which we have committed ourselves and which we are carrying out under a policy which is making gradual progress. The small-scale model seems to me the best solution, even though – as is perhaps regrettable – the material used to make it is often very far removed from the original one.

That is what I wanted very briefly to say about the research we are conducting, which is difficult and tricky and very naturally brings us up against practical financial difficulties and also, it must be admitted, against difficulties of a psychological nature. Our thinking is based on a conviction which we must be able to communicate to others, if we are to enable those with walking, hearing or visual handicaps to have their share, along with other visitors, in the enjoyment of our country's great treasures.

The work of the Commission on the Disabled at the Cité des Sciences et de l'Industrie in Paris, and the Charter for the Disabled

Louis Avan

The Cité des Sciences et de l'Industrie has a somewhat unusual character if we compare it with the more traditional museums, and I think it will be well to draw attention to this. The statutory instrument dated 18 February 1975 by which it was set up states that the Cité is an

> industrial and commercial establishment whose cultural mission is to render progress in sciences, techniques and industrial knowhow accessible to all publics, to broaden the cultural horizon of the men of this country ever more widely to embrace the new prospects afforded by the sciences, the vast field of possible achievements secured by the new technologies, and the changes in outlook introduced into social and economic life by the scientific and technical transformations.

Only recently, in the lecture he gave at La Villette at the meeting of Nobel prizewinners in January 1988, Elie Wiesel spoke of the need to have everyone share in the anxieties and hopes bred of man's ability to avoid the snares ceaselessly laid for him by his own victories. And in the three-year plan which has just been issued for the further development of the Cité des Sciences et de l'Industrie during the period from 1989 to 1992 it is stated: 'All citizens have a right to culture and today more particularly to technological, scientific and industrial culture.' It is further added that 'no stratum of the population must be excluded'.

We have circulated two documents, published respectively in 1982 and 1984. One is entitled *Critères d'accessibilité aux présentations* and is the work of two architects, one of whom, Louis-Pierre Grosbois, is among the contributors to this volume. The other is the *Charter for the Disabled* presented by Paul Delouvrier, the Chairman of the Cité, as a 'directory of the desirable'. We shall be returning to this expression later on.

It should be confessed that the existence of a place as ambitious as the Cité raises problems. There are 30,000 square metres of permanent museum space, plus a multi-media resource centre covering 12,000 square metres (which already has 18,000 volumes and 5,500 subscriptions to periodicals), a highly complex conference centre which raises serious accessibility problems and temporary exhibitions such as the one entitled 'L'Homme réparé' ('Mended Man'); this, in a little under six months, admitted 400,000 visitors, who were able to acquaint themselves not merely with the subject being dealt with but also with the obstacles and limits to genuine accessibility. We must also remember that the declared objective of the Cité is 30,000 visitors per day, and that it has a budget of 4,450 million francs, which would pay for the building of 13 kilometres of motorway and correspond to the value of the buildings and their contents as of June 1984. Furthermore, the Cité envisages breaking out of the ordinary museum framework and becoming a citadel of theatrical entertainment, lectures, debates, workshops and training modules of every kind. As an example I will mention the 'Villette Classes' for deaf or visually handicapped children. All this is a clear reflection of the broadening of the scope of the Cité's mission beyond the limits of the mere museum.

The *Charter for the Disabled* was published as a sequel to the meetings of a working group, ten or so of whose members are among us. These people were chosen by Paul Delouvrier by reason of their direct experience of disablement in themselves or in their family, their profession (architecture for example) or their activity in associations, schools or families in the milieux concerned; their working group has been meeting once a month for eight years now and 75 to 80 per cent of its members regularly attend its meetings. It is not a pressure group; to use Paul Delouvrier's own expression it is a 'vigilance council' which works on a long-term basis and is conscious of the need to distinguish between the ideal and the possible when establishing operational objectives. It concerns itself with the display of the exhibits, with the finding of scientific and technical discoveries for the use of the disabled which may suitably be proposed and with the architectural aspects of accessibility. It must not be forgotten that the Cité des Sciences et de l'Industrie was built on the site of the former slaughterhouse, whose steel structures very seriously restricted the architect's freedom; the fact that they weigh one and a half times as much as the Eiffel Tower will enable you to appreciate some of the difficulties which Louis-Pierre Grosbois may be mentioning. The group also concerns itself with access to information and with what Mr Erlande-Brandenburg has called 'attitudinal' accessibility, by which he means the new way in which all the guide-lecturers and staff in charge at the Cité are called on to look and listen.

The publication of the charter was preceded by a broad discussion at meetings of consultative commissions, each specializing in a given type of disability, and before the text embodying their joint conclusions was drawn up an assessment was made of two pilot events, 'Janus I' and 'Janus II', both held at the request of the President of the Republic. As an example, the best study of a walk-in integrated exhibit depicting the steel industry was provided by a group of a dozen mentally handicapped young people, who had fully grasped the essential approach adopted for an admirably designed theatre which made full allowance for multi-sensory perception. In 1984 Professor Maurice Lévy, a physicist like myself and then the Chairman of the Cité, decided to publish the charter. How has the situation evolved since then? To begin with, the group is continuing its work of assessment and has been reappointed for a further three years under a programme of co-operation instituted by the three-year plan. The next charter will be appended to the three-year plan and will be no longer a catalogue of what is possible but an operational document containing provisions to be respected by architects, designers and all others in charge of developments within the Cité.

Furthermore, new blood is entering the group of thirty: some young disabled people from Marne-la-Vallée have just joined us, and a further group from a hostel for the disabled located near the Cité have annexed the place for themselves and on our behalf they are directly testing its accessibility and its capacity for admitting visitors. These young people are pinpointing possibilities and impossibilities, and with their assistance and that of many other people we have discovered that a number of things which on the face of it appeared to be impossible are not so. This is precisely our role – to detect what is possible and what represents progress.

The new version of the charter is thus going to make due allowance for these tests, for the difficulties we have detected and for the cases of resistance we have sometimes run up against. It is not enough for those in charge to declare their willingness to achieve ideal accessibility and to make of La Villette what Paul Delouvrier has referred to as 'a place exemplary for its accessibility'; such willingness has yet to be the genuine rule in day-to-day life, and above all in the work of the reception staff and of the designers. Here I would like to pay tribute to Ms Adèle Robert for the splendid work she has done in this area for very small children. There remain imperfections, but we are doing our best to iron them out.

An important step was the creation of a permanent unit specifically devoted to accessibility within the Cité. Without trespassing on the pre-rogatives of Hoëlle Corvest, Guy Bouchauveau and others, I would like to emphasize the role of this permanent unit on accessibility as a vehicle for conveying information, as the group's ambassador and above all as a critical assessment and suggestion unit. It is certainly thanks to Guy

Cultural policies concerning disabled people

Bouchauveau and Hoëlle Corvest, for example, that there exist areas for receiving visitors with special needs and it is extremely touching to see people who have no hearing difficulty whatsoever join the groups being taken round by Guy Bouchauveau because his explanations 'speak' directly to everyone, even though he may be primarily addressing himself to people who are deaf.

What I would like to stress in conclusion is the desire of our group to embody this assessment of achievements and this grading of possibilities in the future charter. Mention has been made of exploration by touch. At the Brigitte Fribourg Laboratory of which I have the pleasure of being director, we have just built two machines designed by Leonardo da Vinci. Here is an illustration of the way these things can come about. IBM had mounted an exhibition at Leonardo's house, the Clos-Lucé, in Amboise, illustrating fifty or so fabulous machines selected from among the two hundred and ten designed by the great genius. When we visited the exhibition we found that, contrary to what had been initially claimed, the objects on show could not be fully examined by blind people because it was forbidden to touch them. We therefore decided to take our inspiration from the Clos-Lucé experiment because of its aesthetic qualities but to build several machines of reasonable size so that a blind or visually handicapped person could explore them completely, and to exploit the differences in materials and the fact that these machines could be made to work. The Clos-Lucé machines are static but ours are dynamic; we have already built a very fine system of rods and cranks and an odometer capable of automatically measuring distances travelled.

What I can already say with certainty is that more and more disabled people have adopted the Cité des Sciences et de l'Industrie as a part of their heritage. Naturally there are two areas in which our activity still needs extending; we must reduce the difficulties which still exist in the Cité, and for this purpose we need to be provided with critical analyses. Here I am thinking of the analysis of this sort made by another contributor, Francisco Garcia Aznarez, a highways engineer from Spain. We also need to improve the sensory aids to access, which we feel to be inadequate; the signposting is still disorderly to some extent, with nondescript lettering which is ill-lit and screens often unsuitably placed for those with impaired vision. One comes to realize that whatever is done to improve accessibility from the architectural point of view and from the point of view of the information provided will be helpful to all of us. For example, I came across a text on the principles of the laser which even for physicists would have been completely abstract and partially incomprehensible; it had been initially written by a physicist and then, as it were, passed through a mincing machine from which it had emerged in a form I found incomprehensible, with even mild distortion of one of the principles involved.

Well, I would say it was perfectly possible to give a clear explanation of lasers to mentally handicapped young people, as I have myself made the experiment in a lecture; and if one makes the effort to render the subject accessible to such an audience one can make it accessible to the entire community.

There is a detail which is rather more than a detail; I refer to the part played by the training of the educational staff. And here I would like to pay tribute to all those present here who belong to the accessibility unit, which periodically organizes training programmes for the new arrivals among the educational staff of the Cité.

In closing, I would like to thank once again the Cité des Sciences et de l'Industrie for making such partial accessibility possible and to repeat my thanks to the Fondation de France. It was Nancy Breitenbach who so very exactingly supervised the wire guidance system devised for the 'L'Homme réparé' exhibition and I wish to thank both her and Sylvie Tsyboula for being so strict; progress is impossible otherwise.

I feel that making the Cité accessible to disabled people means first of all making accessible not merely the whole of its scientific content but also its aesthetic qualities – for what is accessible need not necessarily be ugly – and also its potential as a genuine place for mutual contacts and exchanges of the wealth each individual has to offer. And to emphasize the importance of the task of social interaction which the Cité is beginning to fulfil via the works of the many creators to be found among the disabled, I will end by quoting a very fine passage from Diderot's *Letter Concerning the Blind Addressed to Those Who Can See*: 'Listening to the man blind from birth and exchanging impressions with him would have been an occupation not unworthy of the united talents of Locke, Leibnitz and Newton'.

The 'Handicap and Culture' programme at the Fondation de France: a ten-year assessment

Nancy Breitenbach

In the world of the disabled one frequently hears about such basic needs as general assistance and medical care, proper jobs and decent housing. The improvement of the living conditions of disabled people has always been one of the priorities of the Fondation de France: in 1970, very shortly after its creation, it launched a 'generosity crusade' which brought in thirty million francs and made possible the opening of about forty institutions for mentally handicapped children.

We naturally continue to concern ourselves with what is considered to be 'fundamental'. But how about the subject-heading of 'recreational activities' or 'quality of life'? Is cultural life to be considered a luxury?

We do not consider 'culture' to be something superfluous. Nor, we imagine, do you. We all know that it lies at the very heart of human existence.

For the Fondation de France the active participation of the disabled in cultural life is an important, not to say essential, factor in their self-realization and in their integration into the community. And for the past ten years the Fondation has been striving to make artistic and cultural activities available to those who suffer from handicaps. It began by giving its support to art workshops. This activity grew in extent in the years 1982 to 1985 and subsidies were given to a hundred or so associations, to a total amount of over five million francs.

This aspect of 'Handicap and Culture' was very much worth while, and France became one of the leading countries in the area of creative activity for the disabled. The work is now being pursued on a national scale with the formation of the French Committee for Creativity by and with the Handicapped.

However, an assessment of the achievements of these years showed that a programme pursued in this one direction only was raising a certain number of problems. By confining ourselves to catering for the disabled purely as potential artists and treating them as authors of exceptional works we were not doing much to lower the barriers separating them from the rest; on the contrary, we were gradually building the walls of a new ghetto – a ghetto of separate identities and cultural indigence – in which the individual was thrown back on his own resources.

In 1987 we decided that it was essential to tackle the other side of the problem, that of the disabled person as *consumer* of artistic and cultural works in the same way as any other individual. We needed to find the means of giving the disabled access to the cultural premises and cultural events which the able-bodied were free to frequent as they wished. We needed to get round such obstacles as:

- physical inaccessibility
- problems of sense perception
- conceptual understanding
- acceptance by the rest of the public.

It was a huge task, and one whose undertaking called for wise discernment. We needed to take action wherever there were clear signs that conditions were unsuitable for receiving disabled persons and wherever a request for a solution to the problem was making itself heard.

There were three reasons for our decision to focus our efforts on museums.

In the first place there was the discovery, made during the months we had spent preparing our cultural guides to Paris for handicapped persons – a work in which Ms Ecole and Ms Massé, both present here, had a large share – that very many museums remained inaccessible to such persons: 50 per cent of the Paris museums are not in the guides because at the stage when the survey was made they offered no facilities at all to a disabled person, whatever his or her disability.

Second, we also felt that it was the right moment. Indeed we were not alone in turning our attention to the problem. We had met a number of forerunners such as Michel Bourgeois-Lechartier (who will be presenting his findings to this present symposium), Françoise Buchard, of the French Federation of Societies of Friends of Museums, Dominique Hof of the Club VU and others.

Third, the Direction des Musées de France was embarking at the time on an ambitious renovation programme. It was an ideal opportunity not merely to draw attention to the importance of special facilities for users of wheelchairs as provided for by the law passed in 1975 but also to encourage the provision of special equipment and devices enabling people with other sorts of handicap to derive enjoyment from their heritage.

At the same time we came to see that the disabled world was itself expressing the same wishes. Thus the Valentin Haüy Association was holding a competition on the subject of 'Opening the Museums to the Blind' and we were more than happy to join it as an organizer. There was thus no lack of readiness to serve the cause. Some exciting experiments were being made, both in France and abroad, but they remained isolated initiatives. A great many members of the professions concerned expressed their 'desire to do something', but confessed to being held up by two major problems: lack of funds, of course, but, more important still, want of technical information.

That was how the idea of holding this symposium came about. It has two objectives:

1. To inform the maximum number of people on the *philosophy* of opening all types of museums to the disabled, on the specific *requirements* of each kind of disability and on the manifold possible *solutions* to the problem;
2. To spark off new initiatives.

A certain number of projects have already been funded or are now being studied. We may mention the Cité des Sciences et de l'Industrie at La Villette in Paris, the Fine Arts Museum and the Education Museum in Rouen, the Natural History Museum in Nantes and the Paris Museum of Modern Art, all of which are seeking to adapt their premises to enable the handicapped to move around them with greater ease. The Musée Denon at Châlon-sur-Saône is mounting a new tactile exhibition in conjunction with two other provincial museums. Furthermore, we are at present working on the means of funding the purchase of specialized installations for the auditoria of the Pompidou Centre and the Greater Louvre. This is only a beginning. We hope to be able to help a great many other museums to adapt themselves to the requirements of their disabled public. This symposium will therefore be the cornerstone of a long and enthralling campaign.

Changing basic attitudes

Frans Schouten

When someone wants to communicate with an audience he or she has to be aware of the conditions under which the exchange will take place. But unfortunately most museums do not realize the existence of this basic aspect of communication.

When preparing this talk I asked myself how I could properly discuss the problems of disabled people in museums when a lot of so-called 'normal' people feel themselves to be mentally handicapped when they leave a museum, promising themselves that they will never go again to an institution that makes them so uncertain about themselves and so frustrated by the impression that everything is far beyond their intellectual grasp. The accessibility of our cultural heritage is not only a problem for handicapped visitors: although they face some of the same problems as other visitors they have to cope in addition with extra barriers which will make the already difficult task an impossible one.

I am not going to talk to you about all the kinds of facilities we need to establish in our museums and monuments, nor about the specific problems museums have to face if housed in historic buildings, when seeking to adapt their premises to the needs of disabled visitors. I am not going to talk either about how to make a picture gallery accessible to blind people, nor about concerts for deaf people: there are limits to our ability to adapt facilities for everyone. I would like to talk about the attitudes of museum people towards the disabled. This sounds so simple and is yet so complicated. I remember one education officer addressing himself to a group of wheelchair users as though addressing a group of mentally retarded children. The group happened to have an appointment with the curator to talk about a professional matter; but he had seen wheelchairs, claimed them immediately as his protégés, and leapt to a common pre-judgement: disabled people are not normal, so address yourself to them in a very simple way. One could tell a great many similar stories.

Cultural policies concerning disabled people

Where disabled visitors are concerned the attitude of the museum people is an essential factor. I remember a trip to the United States during which I strained my back. I nevertheless wanted to see a lot of museums. But in some of them, when I arrived by taxi, the guards immediately spotted me as a disabled person and came along with a wheelchair, thinking this is the right type of attitude, instead of waiting at the top of the stairs and then politely informing me that they were difficult ones to go up.

The general impression of helplessness is reinforced by the widespread tendency to see disability as an illness. Although members of a disabled persons' consumer organization have observed: 'We are not sick', it is a basic assumption in the medical profession that those whom it serves are 'patients'. The impression of helplessness may also be reinforced by the presuppositions of the social service professions, which find it all too easy to assume that a client incapable of earning his living is also incapable of thinking for himself. Staff members in historical institutions and museums, like people in general, also tend to be confused by many types of disability. On top of this, some people find the sight of physical deformity disturbing, and most people look at the disabled with a certain degree of curiosity.

Some disabled persons prefer to meet the situation head on by bringing up the subject themselves. Others are shy as a result of previous unfortunate experiences. At the same time many able-bodied people are embarrassed because they have had little experience of disabled persons and are uncertain how to react in their presence; they are so anxious not to make mistakes that they may make more mistakes than usual, particularly when performing some unfamiliar task such as pushing a wheelchair.

As a result, museums and historical institutions and their personnel, genuinely eager to help disabled visitors but uncertain how to do so, may hover over them trying to anticipate their needs. That approach may make it difficult for these visitors to do anything for themselves; but most disabled persons will ask for help when they need it. Staff or volunteers need not feel any greater obligation to press help on them than on any other visitors.

At our museological training centre we have two major goals for our students when we train them to receive the disabled. First of all, they must be given a better understanding of the needs, learning modes and shared interests of these visitors, and second they must use that understanding to determine whether the education programmes are effective and appropriate and whether they could be modified.

The training programme is in two phases. We ask students to explore the exhibit floors using devices such as wheelchairs, and blindfolded, in order to simulate a handicapping condition and to be thinking about the exhibits in terms of that condition. This cannot be, and is not intended to be, an activity which simulates what it is like to be handicapped: the last thing we want to hear is 'Now we know what it is like to be handicapped.' You cannot achieve that in an hour and a half. It is an activity which represents, rather, a way of getting students to think about the kind of services and the kind of exhibits which can be made available.

The second phase consists in working with outside handicapped consultants. We hold discussions which deal with specific disabilities and with many myths and misconceptions. The handicapped consultants talk about how they perceive their own disabilities. These are not didactic lectures; they are real give-and-take sessions which I think have been very successful in getting the students to admit some of the concerns and fears they experience when working with disabled people, and they have also come to lay bare some of their misconceptions towards the latter. We have to be aware of the fact that for people who have never been brought face to face with disabled people a first encounter can often represent a threat – a reminder that everyone is vulnerable and that it could happen to anybody any time. Most people do not want to think about that: if you close your eyes to problems you don't have to deal with them.

What we are trying to do is to open the eyes of our students. But the truth of the matter is also that disability is something we have to deal with: we have to do so because by the year 2000 approximately 50 per cent of the people in Europe and in the United States and probably more in the developing countries will in one way or another be disabled; that is a fact of life. People are living longer but they have to live with a disability. These are the realities, and, as I have just said, we have to deal with them. So *we* have to prepare our premises and facilities to face these realities; but first of all we have to prepare ourselves and reshape the attitude of our personnel, and I hope this conference will constitute a worthwhile contribution to such a change of attitude.

II
Funding possibilities

Museums and sponsorship

Roland May

Since 1986 sponsoring has developed in a multitude of different forms. It began by being 'officialized', if I may venture to use the term, when the state took the matter up, its most immediate measures being the enacting of the law passed on 23 July 1987 and the setting-up of a Supreme Council on Cultural Sponsorship composed of managers of firms, officers in charge of cultural services and members of elective assemblies.

I deliberately use the word 'officialize' because it applies here to the recognition of two phenomena which are twin offshoots of sponsorship. The one has consisted in a strengthening of the impact of museums, which, in the past few years, have developed into what may truly be called 'cultural undertakings', their doors wide open to a constantly growing public which is an integral part of our universe of communication. The other is the attempt on the part of private firms to find a cultural brand image expressing itself through financial participation in a variety of cultural initiatives.

Sponsoring has thus developed, and though we are still living through the years of its youth, it is not to be denied that it has achieved a degree of maturity, even though only relative compared with the level reached by our British and American friends.

Examples are naturally numerous and I have no wish to bore you by reading out a list; it will be more expedient to make a few general remarks.

In the first place, it is to be noted that sponsorship operations are not necessarily anything to do with a firm's main activity. This is certainly encouraging in that it signifies diversification of possible sources, but it is also disconcerting for the curator. Indeed most of the applications made, especially by small or medium-sized towns, tend to be made on the initiative of the curators, whose time is valuable, whereas the 'hunt for sponsors' is a slow business.

Funding possibilities

In the second place, the operations undertaken in partnership have become extremely diversified. Whereas the initial reflex was to apply for assistance for the financing of events exploitable by the media, such as exhibitions, the publishing of catalogues, the making of new acquisitions or the holding of receptions, we now find such assistance being used for restoration work, and for lighting, transport and similar museographical requirements. The campaign now being launched by the Fondation de France fits in, in fact, with this wider approach and broadens further still the field of action.

Sponsorship has further taken on a new dimension with appeals for individual contributions – for a sort of 'popular' sponsoring in the best sense of the term. The first such operation permitted the purchase, in 1987, of the *St. Thomas*, painted by Georges de La Tour, and other similar appeals have followed, for example, the one recently launched in Marseilles with a view to awakening public opinion to the importance of preserving works of art. It has thus become clear from several years' experience that such co-operation produces results. The success of museums is being bought at a price, which is the increasingly high cost of the architectural work, the purchase of exhibits and so on. Financial support is not merely welcome; it also enables individuals to express their interest in the running of such institutions in concrete form.

But this paper would not be complete without mention of the reservations made – and this, I feel, is significant – at once by associations of sponsors (such as Admical, the Association pour le développement du ménécat industriel et commercial, to give only one example) and by members of the museum professions. These reservations concern the actual philosophy of sponsorship. In no case must the private funding be treated as a means of 'tiding over' the Ministry of Culture or the local authorities. The expression was first used by Jacques Rigaud, and we heartily endorse it. The role of the state and of the local authorities must remain predominant: sponsoring is an auxiliary measure and an incitement to explore yet further potential initiatives. Here again the scheme proposed by the Fondation de France is exemplary as an illustration of what can be done.

It is paradoxical that the distortion of this philosophy should have been the work of the state. We have often felt that the kind of sponsorship officialized by the Ministry in 1987 was part of a policy of 'state-controlled liberalism'. The state was not to confine itself to devising fiscal measures or to encouraging the sponsors to determine the rules of the game; this is made clear, particularly in the provisions governing joint financing and in the institution of the Supreme Sponsorship Council. The granting of public subsidies was to be dependent on the effective *prior* collection of private funds. The desire of the government was to give private firms a greater measure of initiative, but it reflected a misconception of everyday realities and threw to the winds three centuries of centralized practice. For many of us, in effect, private financial aid was, on the contrary, necessarily dependent on prior commitment by the state. Furthermore, since the applications submitted to the Council have frequently come from small or medium-sized museums, the sums involved have been modest and have even seemed ridiculously so to the Council members. But this is merely a reflection of the realities of the French museum world, composed as it is of over two thousand museums varying greatly in size and in scale of impact and in the degree of interest attaching to them. The measure in question is in fact at present being reviewed in so far as it applies to museums. A further point is that increased encouragement of systematic recourse to sponsorship – in certain areas at least – has led to keener competition and to the need for applications to be prepared in an increasingly professional manner.

I felt it was essential to pass these few observations on to you for the purposes of this collection arising from the symposium on museums and the disabled.

In any sponsoring scheme allowance must always be made for the individual identity of the museum and for its socio-economic context; too often the big operations widely popularized by the media have masked more complex realities. In a town of medium size which is prepared to improve the services it offers to the disabled an operation costing ten or fifty thousand francs will have the same relative effect as the larger operation a major town may be prepared to subsidize for a larger population.

I trust, then, that the initiative of the Fondation de France will be fully approved by curators and by the authorities, that the General Association of Curators will support it by circulating particulars of the measures envisaged and the procedure to be adopted and that the Fondation will treat all projects submitted to it with an equal amount of interest.

Jacques Rigaud has said that 'sponsorship must be earned'. I fully agree with him, and I would add that the success of sponsorship will be the outcome of a regular dialogue and of mutual understanding between the parties to the enterprise.

The Fondation de France as sponsor

Sylvie Tsyboula

I am going briefly – and somewhat anecdotally – to talk to you about the Fondation de France, both as a body in the service of sponsorship and as a 'collective' sponsor in its own right. Sponsoring, for us, does not mean merely the operations on the part of firms about which we have heard so much in the past few years; it also – and I would even say primarily – means sponsoring by individuals.

How did the Fondation de France come into existence, and how, under its constitution, can it thus serve the cause of sponsorship?

When our organization was founded in 1969 the prime movers were a great minister and a great president. André Malraux, as General de Gaulle's Minister of Culture, was seeking the means of setting up in France some sort of foundation resembling the cultural foundations of the US model. In short, he wanted something of a great, rich and powerful kind. He sent a member of the Council of State to the United States, but the latter brought back the constitutions of the Community Trusts, which are charitable institutions, set up in individual towns, and which do not run on the same lines as the larger Foundations, such as the Rockefeller. They began to flourish on the other side of the Atlantic after the First World War as the expression, in the form of assistance to the most impoverished members of the population, of the gratitude felt by the notabilities of the big towns for their own good fortune. These notabilities donated money to a fund set up by a group of other notabilities among their friends with the idea that the interest on their donations should go to heal the sufferings of widows, orphans and old or disabled people, or to further the upkeep of the parks in the town.

In reality the Community Trusts are based on a number of extremely simple concepts: a board of well-known and honourable public figures, and funds which represent the aggregate formed by individual contributions, on the principle that little streams make great rivers. The aim of all this is to serve the interests of the town's population, and the background to it all is the hope that such generous intentions will go on for ever and ever, with boards of trustee citizens succeeding each other to ensure both the proper management of the funds entrusted to them and the achievement of the objectives in the general interest. We find ourselves here in a cultural and civic environment peculiarly American: those who have been successful are indebted both for their merits and for their good fortune to the poorest and least well-to-do. In the American context, the state and the public institutions play a far smaller part than in France in education, medical care, welfare services and protection of the individual. Yet when we come to look at it the Fondation de France is roughly speaking a community trust.

Article One of our Constitution shows that we are primarily in the service of our donors. It states:

> The institution known as the Fondation de France has as its aim the receiving of all bounties, notably in the form of donations, legacies or cash payments, the management of the said funds and the redistribution of the same or of the income or product deriving therefrom for the benefit of persons, charities or philanthropic, educational, scientific, social or cultural institutions serving the general interest, with due regard for such intentions, obligations and conditions as may have been stipulated by the donors.

This is what we call the work of 'receiving and serving the donors'. And, year in, year out, we function very much in the same way as a community trust. Like the trusts of the big American towns, we have a board composed partly of the heirs – or rather of the successors – of the original subscribers of funds, which were private or public banks. It should be realized that, though its name might suggest otherwise, the Fondation de France is a private institution whose initial capital was subscribed by seventeen public or private financial institutions. One section of the board of governors is thus composed of representatives of these banks, and a further section of experts who represent the various French ministries concerned with the general interest (education, health, young people's welfare). The other third consists of outside public figures co-opted on their own merits and differing as widely in sphere of activity as – for example – Professor Jean Bernard of the Academy of Sciences and the historian and novelist Françoise Chandernagor.

The Fondation de France was also set up – and here we are in a context typically French – to fill a gap left by the law. Under French law no one can, merely by making a will to that effect, set up a foundation for the purpose of leaving his property to a cause, declaring, for example: 'I leave my goods to the blind.' That will not suffice to create a foundation for the intended purpose; but if the legacy is made to the Fondation de France to enable the latter to create the foundation this will be perfectly feasible.

I imagine Article One of our Constitution will have partially enlightened you on the range of widely differing services we are able to render. Since we are at the service of the donors for the receipt of 'all bounties' in a variety of forms and for redistribution of 'the income . . . deriving therefrom' for the benefit of any and every sort of institution serving the general interest, we work in accordance with each individual request. Thus the Fondation de France may create a foundation coming under its own authority, or may pass on a legacy to an association, a library or a research laboratory or any other such general interest body, or else may merely help a donor to invent some generous use for his money for which there has previously been no equivalent. We are permitted to 'imagine' such arrangements, and I believe this is the Fondation de France's greatest blessing: since it is independent of the state and of the administration, in the service of its donors but authorized, should they be still alive, to help them think about the possibilities, it is able to innovate. This is one of our peculiar features, and it keeps us in a sort of dynamic tension in relation to the wishes of these donors. If they are still alive things are easy, for we can discuss things with them. If they are dead, we are obliged, first and foremost, to abide by what they have said in their wills. There are, for example, donors who wished to do something after their death in the general interest and on behalf of a given category of distressed members of the population; but how can the Fondation de France make the best possible use today of sums left to it twenty years ago for the benefit – for example – of tubercular children? There are not as many tubercular patients in France today as might be supposed, and the treatment is not the same as might have been given twenty or so years ago. The instructions left must therefore be brought up to date, and this is to a great extent what makes our work so interesting.

I will now take a look at the other aspect of the task of the Fondation, which consists in acting collectively as sponsor. For though our Constitution in a sense made of us a body to which sponsors and donors, whether individuals or firms, were to address themselves, something still needed to be done in the initial stages, when no such funds were available.

When the Fondation was set up in 1969, we were tempted to take immediate action, and this is the reason why its first two operations involved both fund-raising and public-awareness campaigns. In 1970 the Fondation, with the backing of the state and the relevant big associations, organized a gigantic campaign to popularize the cause of the mentally disabled. In those days mentally disabled people were kept shut up inside their homes because it was not known how to look after them, and above all because people were ashamed of taking them out. In 1975 we organized another campaign on rather similar lines to draw attention to the loneliness of old people. The position was much the same: people were not yet used to seeing grandfathers and grandmothers make their sprightly descent from motorcoaches on their sightseeing jaunts to the four corners of the earth. Those were the days when an old person was thought to have more than one foot in the grave.

And so, little by little, the Fondation de France has discovered a means of action and acquired its present personality, which makes it a sort of welfare pioneer counting on the support of 350,000 donors. When we speak of collective sponsorship we are referring to these 350,000 people who every year make us a smaller or larger donation, the average amount being 260 francs; such donations are 'semi-earmarked', which means that they are to be used 'for the disabled', 'for culture', etc. This leaves us a certain amount of elbow room, which, once again, means that we can try to innovate.

I will conclude by drawing attention to what Mr Roland May has just said about the relative effect of operations. It seems perfectly normal, for example, for the walls of an X-ray room in Manchester to be painted blue, but doubtless such an idea would be completely new in the depths of the Spanish countryside and it is practically unknown in rural areas in France. Innovations are extremely relative things. When an institution such as the Fondation de France gives some of you the opportunity of telling your everyday experiences, it must be realized that for others such everyday phenomena are totally revolutionary. One of our tasks is to provide, in addition to a bit of money, a great deal of information; this is a new kind of sponsorship, consisting in facilitating relations between different branches of society, and different 'levels' of perception of reality – between those who are better and those who are less well informed.

The Carnegie United Kingdom Trust: the ADAPT Fund

It is quite clear from knowledge of existing arts venues that the majority are not in every sense accessible to the range of people with disabilities. The cost of upgrading every venue primarily concerned with the arts would be enormous and in many cases it would be impracticable to make the venue fully accessible. Nevertheless, all concerned are agreed that there is an overwhelming argument for a national Adaptations Fund, to achieve the greatest possible accessibility. The objectives of such a Fund are:

1. To challenge venue owners and managers to think about essential improvements and plan for these within their resources, augmented if approved from the Fund.
2. To ensure improvements as models of good practice.
3. By use of challenge grants to encourage additional, and at least equal financial resources from local communities.

Without a challenge Fund, further improvements in accessibility will be achieved only slowly and will not necessarily be satisfactory, if the least expensive solution to each problem has to be sought, at the expense of quality.

These are the reasons why the Carnegie United Kingdom Trust has offered £250,000 on condition of a similar contribution from other sources to establish the Fund. It is not the Carnegie Trustees' policy to give grants for buildings or adaptation generally, but they have done so on this occasion because they are convinced of the right of disabled people to share fully in the arts − a right which they are being denied as long as physical obstacles and negative attitudes persist.

The drive was launched in London in September 1989 by the Carnegie United Kingdom Trust to give challenge grants to those willing to adapt their premises for these potential 'customers'. Matching funds have been received from the Ministry for the Arts, local authorities, charitable trusts and commerce.

The Fund for the Arts venue improvements programme is called ADAPT (Access for Disabled People to Arts Premises Today), '... because that is exactly what we want people to do – to make changes and alterations so that a whole section of our population frozen out of culture can also join in the great wealth of arts in this country', said Mr Geoffrey Lord, Secretary of the Carnegie United Kingdom Trust.

ADAPT is not an endowment or investment fund. The aim is to utilize the capital as quickly as possible for essential improvements such as ramps, handrails, lifts, appropriately designed toilets, induction loop-hearing systems, appropriate seating, signposting. There will be other forms of improvements and, indeed, it is hoped that the availability of matching funding will be a stimulus to imaginative thinking about access on condition that these ideas respect appropriate standards, e.g. lifts of correct size to allow movement of a wheelchair, correct height of telephone, etc.

The assistance is restricted to the physical improvements or adaptations of premises; applications cannot be considered for actual work already commenced or completed and grants will not be made retrospectively.

The creation of the new ADAPT Fund is but the latest of a long record of projects which in Carnegie's own words aim to 'improve the well-being of masses of people'. It is also one of the biggest ventures the Trust has ever undertaken in this country, in co-operation with government, other trusts and companies.

III
Museums and physical disabilities

Adapting historic buildings to make them accessible to the disabled

Francisco García Aznarez

In Spain today, 50 per cent of the amounts allocated to building work are used for restoration. As most of the places restored are museums, administrative offices and other public buildings, advantage must be taken of the operations in progress to do away with barriers to accessibility.

Architects and engineers effectively show a degree of willingness to avoid erecting such barriers in new buildings, but none at all to do away with them in buildings that already exist, either for practical reasons or through incapacity. As an excuse they invoke purportedly insuperable technical or economic difficulties or the impossibility of conforming to the regulations, especially in the case of buildings of historical interest.

In 1986 I brought out a small work describing the restoration of a large number of buildings, many of them historical monuments. Without going into too many details I will say this much here:

1. All the equipment required for solving the technical difficulties is readily available on the market; all that are required are capable professionals. The main problem where accessibility is concerned is that of movement from one floor to the other, and there now exist all sorts of lifts and platforms for the purpose.

2. I worked out the cost of removing barriers in three different ways. Let us take, for example, the question of vertical accessibility. If we base ourselves on the maxima we shall allow for the cost of all the lifts (or other means of access), and if on the minima we shall allow only for that of the means of access specifically designed for the disabled. If we take the mean figures we shall replace an air-conditioned lift by a non-air-conditioned one and the cost of the aids for the disabled will be deducted from the resultant savings. The result obtained by calculating on the basis of these last-mentioned criteria will be as shown in Figure 1. The *y*-axis will give us the cost of the removal of barriers to

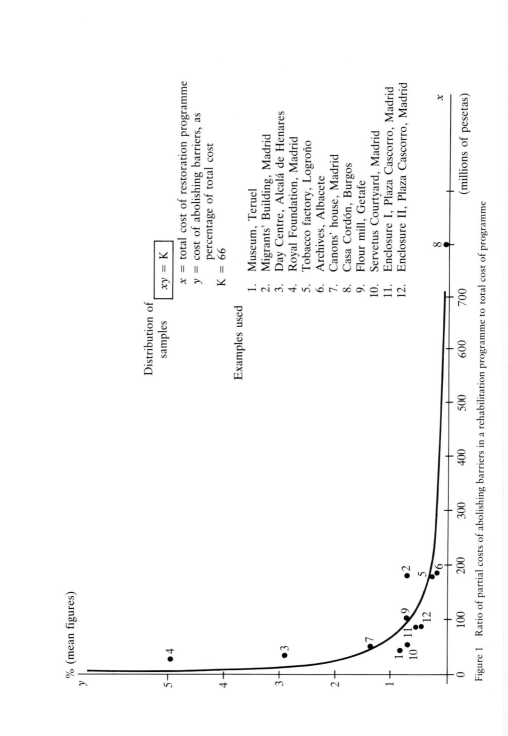

Distribution of samples $xy = K$

x = total cost of restoration programme
y = cost of abolishing barriers, as percentage of total cost
$K = 66$

Examples used

1. Museum, Teruel
2. Migrants' Building, Madrid
3. Day Centre, Alcalá de Henares
4. Royal Foundation, Madrid
5. Tobacco factory, Logroño
6. Archives, Albacete
7. Canons' house, Madrid
8. Casa Cordón, Burgos
9. Flour mill, Getafe
10. Servetus Courtyard, Madrid
11. Enclosure I, Plaza Cascorro, Madrid
12. Enclosure II, Plaza Cascorro, Madrid

Figure 1   Ratio of partial costs of abolishing barriers in a rehabilitation programme to total cost of programme

accessibility expressed as a percentage of the total cost of the restoration work, and the x-axis will give us the total cost in millions of pesetas. The curve obtained will be an equilateral parabola.

With 50,000 French francs we can reduce the obstacles in almost all existing buildings at minimum cost – at an absurdly low figure. Naturally if all the individual cases are to be fully dealt with a larger investment will be needed; in Spain we evaluate this at 1 per cent of the total budget.

3. The Spanish regulations governing the protection of buildings, which used to be extremely rigid, have been relaxed and architects can no longer use this pretext to conceal their incompetence.

The conclusion to be drawn from this exploratory work is clear: there is no insuperable obstacle to the removal of barriers to accessibility. There is merely timidity, or lack of professionalism in the trades concerned, over and above the difficulties inherent in any restoration work. A very considerable effort must therefore be made to see that the people in these trades are properly informed.

The needs of people with walking handicaps. The Association des Paralysés de France

Pascal Dubois

If there are so many of us here at this symposium, this is doubtless because we are unanimous in recognizing that the disabled, too, are entitled to have access to culture and to enjoyment of their leisure. A change of scenery, entertainment, self-realization, an escape from the routine of the never-ending days, the ability to forget the day-to-day problems without help from other people and to feel mentally at ease – such are the aspirations of those disabled people who are convinced today that the way to genuine integration lies in part through culture and leisure pursuits.

The essential factors to be borne in mind for purposes of our work here today are:

- the material facilities
- information
- human assistance.

Personally I shall be dealing more particularly with the technical aspect of the material facilities. On premises to which the public are admitted people with walking handicaps still too often come up against a certain number of obstacles. Yet there are ways of overcoming these, and my purpose is to describe them to you. I am going to give you an account of the 'logical' itinerary for a person with a walking handicap, from outside the building (or in actual fact from the parking area) to the inside.

It should first of all be explained that as regards accessibility there are regulations in France which distinguish new buildings from those previously in existence. And I think it is important to state exactly what is meant by 'accessibility'. Statutory Instrument N° 78–109 dated February 1978 (Article 4) gives in my opinion a definition genuinely reflecting the needs of the persons concerned. Thus premises are considered to be accessible to disabled persons with a walking handicap in all cases where they afford such persons, particularly those who must constantly use a wheelchair, the possibility of entering, moving freely from one point to another once inside, leaving again under normal conditions of convenience, and taking advantage of all the services offered to the public.

Who are the users directly confronted by the problems connected with accessibility? They are those who are obliged to use a wheelchair or walking sticks, old people, parents pushing prams, etc. We should add to these, if we are to complete the list of those in the 'walking handicap' category, children, pregnant women and people temporarily disabled.

It is important to realize that accessibility is undeniably an unbroken succession of stages. It starts at the point where the car is parked (which must be as near as possible to the building) and must be taken to mean accessibility for everyone to all the services provided or benefits granted to the public whatever these may be, and to all the rooms in the building. Each new set of premises must be designed with a view to giving full autonomy to those visiting it, even though in fact some of them may not be able to forgo the assistance of another person.

There is no doubt whatever that an access at street level is the ideal arrangement in that it does away with the need for special itineraries or installations and hence with the burden on the community which would derive from extra expenditure. Where a special way in for people with walking handicaps needs to be devised in existing buildings (as frequently happens in museums) it should be as near as possible to the main thoroughfare used by everyone else. Frequently, in effect, we find special entrances which have been intelligently designed being used by all and sundry.

The entrance hall is an important place of transit from which all visitors must be able to enter the museum and in which they should be able to find all and any data capable of facilitating their movements. Notice boards must always be legible for people who are seated, and should therefore not be above 1.6 metres from the ground. Disabled people must also be able to reach the necessary levels at counters, information desks and ticket offices without systematically needing the help of an extra person; here again, there must be a regulation maximum height (from 0.2 to 1.6 metres from the ground for devices needing to be reached, and from 0.4 to 1.4 metres for anything to be grasped with the hand).

If there are automatic devices to be worked by the visitor as live exhibits – as at the Cité des Sciences et de l'Industrie in Paris or at the Futuroscope in Poitiers – they must be accessible to everyone, including those with walking handicaps. Allowance must therefore be made for the levels to which their hands and eyes can reach. The same precaution must be taken in the case of showcases and all printed information. So far as possible all movement within the building should be at ground level, or where this is not possible – in existing buildings – platform lifts should be installed. In addition, all levels should be connected by means of a lift which anyone is free to work (i.e. which is accessible to all alike), and in this the control buttons must be at the right height (i.e. not more than 1.3 metres from the floor).

Where there are such amenities as eating places, for example, people with walking handicaps must be able to reach and use them in the normal run of things, in the same way as all other comers. The same applies to bookshops, information centres, lecture halls, etc.

At least one WC for each sex should be specially adapted for the use of the disabled, especially the wheelchair users; but there is no need to restrict these to their exclusive use, as is still too often the case. 'Adapted' has never been a synonym of 'reserved'. The seat must be accessible from the front or side, preferably the latter, since this is very often more convenient for the people concerned. Arm rests, too, are always welcome since they ensure optimum security during the change of position. Wash-basins likewise must be usable by everyone, as must the devices dispensing soap, paper, hand-towels and other accessories.

Lastly, while it is true that the solving of accessibility problems will involve attention to architectural features, overwhelming importance will also attach to awareness on the part of the reception services staff: the latter must know how to receive and direct all comers.

The accessibility of any building is to be gauged by the extent to which it may be used by people unable to walk normally. The best way of achieving the desired end in this respect – apart from observing the regulations in force – is to acquaint oneself with the handicap of such people and with its implications in everyday life. It would therefore be wise to consult them when thinking of future buildings and of alterations to existing ones.

I have been speaking here as a representative of the Accessibility Department of the Association des Paralysés de France. This body, founded in 1933, officially 'recognized to be in the public interest' in 1945 and approved as a 'national association for popular education' by the Ministry of Young People and Sports in 1959, today has 70,000 members, 14 regional offices, 95 local offices in the 'départements' and 130 institutions. Its aims are as follows:

1. To interest itself in (or actually promote) any initiative designed to improve the moral and material living conditions of the disabled.
2. To assist individual cases through its local offices, its specialized welfare service, its institutions and its other services.
3. To publicize the needs of people with walking handicaps and to vindicate their rights.
4. To bring home their needs to the authorities.
5. To take action to secure suitable legislation.
6. To promote integration in all areas, etc.

The Accessibility Department has been in existence since 1986. Its work consists essentially in:

1. Creating awareness among the population as a whole on problems connected with accessibility, whether they affect places or people.
2. Setting up our own network but also bringing in architects, developers, financiers and all others concerned with building work.
3. Offering the necessary technical advice.
4. Ensuring that the action we take or instigate is duly followed up.
5. Publishing and circulating all technical literature capable of making for enhanced accessibility.

Ever since it was set up, this department, which functions on a national scale, has been taking effective action in such widely differing areas as employment, housing, transport, school education, recreational activities, etc.

Within our Association there are a large number of groups organizing activities which are increasingly anxious to have regular access to cultural and recreational institutions. I would like to stress here that all those who have had the opportunity of visiting the Cité des Sciences et de l'Industrie at La Villette have been fully satisfied with their visit, since the premises they found there were fully accessible and they were able to take the same advantage as anyone else of the various amenities and services offered.

Let us hope that other museums and other cultural institutions may be inspired by this achievement. There is no doubt whatsoever that this is what the disabled are waiting for.

and more generally to fresh implementation of the scheme designed to improve environmental and living conditions.

Pursuant to the reform of the university syllabuses for engineers and architects instituted under the directives issued by the European Community, the aforesaid experts emphasize the need to organize, in this area, specialization courses and systems for the publicizing of basic data on the elimination of architectural barriers and on safety in buildings.

They wish to see the establishment of projects designed to permit the finding of totally new solutions to the problems of security, well-being and the accessibility of public buildings and of towns.

They also wish to see instituted PhD research programmes, specialization courses and documentation centres, the data provided by which would be available to members of the professions in private practice and to engineers and technicians employed by the public authorities and by the major firms belonging to the sector concerned.

Lastly, they wish to see the necessary funds for the financing of the initiatives for bringing projects in this area in line with present-day conditions duly provided by the local authorities (municipal, provincial and regional) in charge of supervising and monitoring new building programmes, in order to increase the responsibility of the experts in respect of the existing legislation.

They request that an initiative be taken in the direction both of the University and of the secondary schools, with a view in particular to specialization courses in the fields of architecture, regional planning and the environment.

Shortly after this European seminar for architects in Milan, I attended a European conference in Utrecht on the accessibility of buildings open to the public. The purpose of this meeting was to suggest European political initiatives designed to harmonize existing measures or to permit the taking of new ones in connection with accessibility in Europe.

The working group under François Vittecoq has proposed an overall accessibility policy overstepping the limits of the concept of architectural barriers to be removed and introducing the notions of access and use for the various publics and for persons working in and near the buildings.

It is proposed, in view of the EEC directives, that all new buildings meet the accessibility criteria for the granting of building permits, and that the proposed provisions entail formal undertakings by the state and by the authorities granting the permits, as well as by developers, designers and contractors.

This same working group calls for harmonization of the minimum accessibility rules in force in each of the member countries of the European Community, and, in the light of a recent Italian law, it has been suggested that the funds and subsidies allocated by the Community, the state and the other public authorities – whether regional or local – should in future be granted only after monitoring of the projects concerned for compliance with accessibility standards.

The report drawn up by this working group naturally proposes that all training courses for future members of the architectural professions should hereafter provide data on the overall accessibility policy.

Hence to preclude wastage of the work of several years, I now propose that there be organized, at the Faculty of Architecture in Milan, a European course on accessibility open to all architects and engineers of EEC member countries. I hope the Commission of the European Communities will approve this proposal and give it its support. In Milan I spoke of a Europe without frontiers, and hence without barriers, and I deliberately use this expression once again, since the European Community of twelve countries, with a population of three hundred and twenty million, must effectively be a Europe without barriers for disabled people – a Europe widely thrown open to admit all disabilities without any exception whatsoever, open to all European citizens.

who had a club foot, 'enjoyed swimming and diving; his infirmity ceased to be a handicap'. This implies that the handicap may be removed by the milieu and provides us with the basic principle that it occurs where the interior of a building is designed in a way unsuited to the individual concerned. In other words, it is the architectural design and the planning of the premises inside which create the handicap or do away with it. This is in fact the position of the World Health Organization, which considers that the disability is a personal feature of the individual whereas the handicap is the social consequence of the disability.

Methodology

Let us now see how we can arrive at a methodology for putting our principles into practice. There are, first of all, the basic principles concerning collective use, i.e. accessibility for all by reason of an overall design which does away with handicaps.

In the case in point the public building is the Cité des Sciences et de l'Industrie in the La Villette district in Paris, itself a rehabilitated building – a science museum housed in what was formerly one of the biggest slaughterhouses in Europe. The building is immense: 270 metres long, 120 metres wide and 40 metres high; its ground-floor area thus covers 30,000 square metres, or four times as much as the Pompidou Centre. It lies inside a park designed to receive cultural institutions, located in between the centre of Paris and its eastern suburbs, between the Porte de La Villette and Porte de Pantin; the park so far contains a museum and a big exhibition hall and is shortly to contain an academy of music, and all these buildings are to be totally accessible.

If we are to explain these results we must here recall a few dates marking the stages in the application of the methodology adopted. In 1979 there was officially set up a public institution under the title of Parc de La Villette, with Paul Delouvrier as its Chairman. In 1980 the architect Adrien Fainsilber was the successful candidate chosen to design the building. Between 1981 and 1983, two commissions were at work, one being the already existing Commission des Associations de Personnes Handicapées and the other being composed of Paul Sautet, Adriana Arameida and myself; Paul Delouvrier as Chairman had decided that the whole project must be exemplary, or in other words he had taken the expression 'going still further' quite literally. Thus between 1981 and 1983 we worked in an advisory capacity with Adrien Fainsilber on accessibility problems. Then from 1983 to 1987 we pursued our co-operation, this time with the team under Jacques Lichnerowicz which

Figure 3   Small electric vehicles are available for people who tire easily

was concerned with the museological aspects – the mounting of the exhibitions and their contents.

Our work basically consisted in the provision of design criteria in the light of which the architects could devise their solutions to the problems. For this purpose we tried to make use of ergonomics – which I prefer to call by the more significant English expression, 'human factors'; by this I mean the technology of communication concerned with the study and further improvement of man's relations with his work from the physio-

Museums and physical disabilities

logical and psychological point of view, or in this instance of *the relations between the visitor and what he is shown in the museum*. This method brings us to the very heart of our objective, which is to further integration into the life of the community by abolishing handicaps caused by indoor facilities and fixtures and by treating all such fittings and arrangements as means of communication.

Figure 4   To enable blind people to circulate, a guiding path of highly contrasted textures has been installed

To enable this method to be applied we defined Rules of Visual and Bodily Accessibility for all the installations, the three basic concepts of which are: Moving, Seeing, Handling.

Moving

Vertically, either by elevator or escalator; both are located in the same area so as to keep the visitors together (Figure 2).
Horizontally: elimination of all obstacles for those who move on wheels and provision of mechanical ramps to and from the car parks.

But also:

■ Small electric vehicles are available for people who tire easily; they are deliberately designed not to look like wheelchairs (see Figure 3).

Figure 5   From their specially designed pushchair, lent by the museum, the youngest visitors can see displays exhibited at ground level

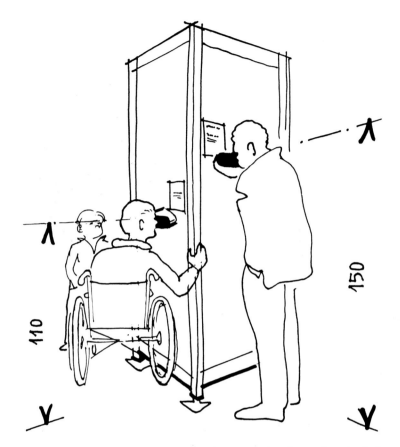

Figure 6   Take into account different heights of visitors with a choice of two levels for viewfinders

- Infants' pushchairs, specially designed for the museum, are also available.
- Where displays are on elevated platforms, short ramps have been built.
- To enable blind people to circulate independently, floor coverings of highly contrasted textures have been used to make a guiding path one metre wide, with a sound signal at crossroads (Figure 4).

Seeing

For all, at the right height. A standing child sees on the same level as an adult in a wheelchair.

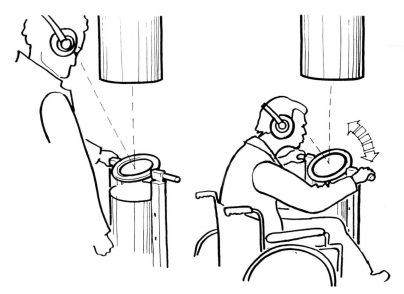

Figure 7   Take into account different heights of visitors with rotating mirrors

But also:

- From their pushchair the youngest visitors can see elements exhibited right down to the ground (Figure 5).
- Devices such as inclined exhibits, mobile viewfinders with a choice of two viewing levels (1.10m or 1.50m) take into account the different heights of visitors (Figures 6 and 7).
- Medium-height, non-glare, vertical showcases and the size and contrast of characters for texts, chosen for their readability.

Handling

For all. Many museum exhibits are 'interactive', i.e. the visitor must handle them in order to obtain information. It was important that they be designed so as to be accessible to all.

Taking the sitting position as a position of reference for all visitors, we succeeded in fully integrating disabled persons in wheelchairs (Figure 8). On this basis, we designed a handling console with a turning seat which

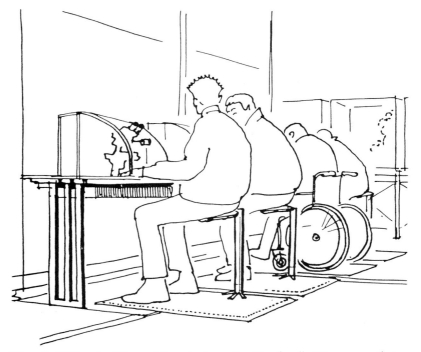

Figure 8   Taking the sitting position as 'reference' position for all visitors ensures that disabled people are fully integrated

pulls aside to make room for a wheelchair. The exhibit operating commands are set at an average height, or at two different heights.

In addition to observing the Rules of Accessibility and to incorporating them into the installations, we tried to make the able-bodied children aware of the problems of the disabled by means of games such as:

- A tactile maze which must be travelled through with closed eyes.
- Steps which must be climbed with stiffened legs (Figure 9).

This is yet another way of proving that architecture can either provoke a disablement or make it disappear.

Twenty centuries ago, the Roman architect Vitruve defined architecture as being an art which answered three needs, *Commoditas, Firmitas, Voluptas* – 'commodity, construction, aesthetics'.

When, therefore, a museum cannot receive a public of any age, with or without a disablement, it is not complying with one of the basic rules of architectural conception: commodity.

Figure 9   In the Inventorium, games such as walking with stiffened legs help children to understand

Insistence upon this basic necessity of architecture, *commodity*, should be one of the essential objects of training for architects and construction professionals.

Accessibility at the Greater Louvre, Paris

C. C. Pei

When people talk about accessibility for the disabled they are usually referring to the 'traditional' disabled – those who use wheelchairs. But we have also made provision for invalids and for elderly people who have difficulty in going up steps or walking long distances. Accessibility problems affect a public much larger than the public actually using wheelchairs, though of course the case of the latter is the most dramatic.

Some of the accessibility problems facing the disabled in museums face everyone else as well, and we need to do as much as we can to improve all means of access to existing buildings. Safety precautions must naturally be taken for all visitors, and, here again, we must bear the disabled in mind, since in the event of an emergency they will face more problems than the rest.

We have tried to improve the system for enabling visitors to find their way about the museum. A disabled person who has taken the wrong direction will have far more trouble in returning to the starting point than will an able-bodied one. The signposting must thus be improved and visitors must at the same time be able to know exactly where they are; even if one is not disabled it is easy to get lost and to start feeling anxious.

The Louvre is perhaps the world's largest museum, or will be so, if this is not the case today, in five years' time when we have completed the second stage in the work on the 'Greater Louvre' and thus increased the total area of exhibition space by 80 per cent.

But the Louvre is also a palace, which began as a fortress and then underwent a series of alterations and additions from the twelfth century onwards, ultimately becoming a royal residence. This raises problems – of level, for example – in more or less all parts of the building. It is also a historical monument, and there are naturally rooms which must be preserved as they are, since they embody a history. Finally, the Louvre also forms part of one of the world's biggest urban complexes.

Allowance must be made for these three factors if we wish to deal with the case of the disabled. The Louvre's position as a feature of its urban context, for example, raises certain problems. Until very recently it formed a sort of barrier between the left and right banks, owing to the fact that the Ministry of Finance occupied the northern part of the buildings. To improve the access from one bank to the other we were anxious to retain all the thoroughfares at ground levels and we have added a passage leading from the Palais-Royal underground station to the pyramid. The problem lies in the fact that the preservation of the accesses at ground level means that all visitors, on arriving at the museum, must either go up and then down again or vice versa, which is particularly hard for disabled people. We felt, however, that fidelity to original design took precedence over individual problems. But we have naturally attempted to provide suitable arrangements for dealing with each of these cases. We have, furthermore, made an underpass of the Avenue du Général Lemonnier so as to enable pedestrians to reach the Louvre directly at ground level from the Tuileries gardens.

Previously a person in a wheelchair could enter the Louvre only on the colonnade side, the main entrance being inaccessible owing to the steps. But now the pyramid can be entered at ground level. A lift and escalators communicate with the main entrance hall 8.5 metres below, and from there all departments may be reached from three points by staircase, escalator or lift. From inside the pyramid one has a excellent view of all the outside walls of the palace, so that one knows exactly where one is. The location of the three means of access to the exhibition galleries are indicated by the three small pyramids.

On the north side we are going to renovate the Ministry of Finance buildings, which will be devoted to paintings, objets d'art, sculpture and oriental antiquities. The Duc de Morny's salon and the big reception rooms will be open to the public. All levels and all areas will be fully accessible to disabled visitors, as there will be six or seven lifts. On the south side we have put in lifts connecting with the present museum, and to the east the visitor has direct access to the department of Egyptian antiquities.

The earliest part of the museum is the twelfth-century Philippe Auguste moat, recently excavated. This, and the fourteenth-century Charles V moat, may be visited by everyone.

Museums and physical disabilities

During the coming twenty years almost all the works in the museum are to be moved and will subsequently be shown to better advantage in their new setting.

Accessibility at the Musée d'Orsay, Paris

Jean-Paul Philippon

At the time when this museum was designed there were three things to be taken into account: the building was a former railway station, works were to be displayed there and they were to be displayed to a public. But I shall be considering the Musée d'Orsay more specifically from the point of view of relations with the public – with how we sought, when turning a station into a museum, to produce something more congenial to the public than most museums, which would have a more friendly atmosphere and be more accessible to every sort of public.

The Gare d'Orsay was the only Paris station to have been built in the central part of the town, inside a residential unit, and the building consists of a big central nave, formerly containing the arrival and departure platforms, plus the structures designed to conceal the fact that it was a station, especially from visitors to the Tuileries gardens. There is a broad lateral façade with two pavilions, designed to match the Louvre. Such was the project issued in 1897 and executed by Victor Laloux for the Great Exhibition in 1900. The part of the buildings looking on to the small square at the end of the Rue de Bellechasse contained the offices and reception lounge of the hotel, while the hotel proper, with its bedrooms, was a very long thin building looking on to the Rue de Lille. When we came to work on the new design we found the big glass roofs and the coffered ceilings still in position.

The essential interest attaching to such a place lies in the fact that it has excellent daylighting, and we attempted to exploit this to the best possible advantage for the museum. At the same time, the huge extent of the available space was a natural incitement to treat relations with the public in an original way: the usual series of galleries could be designed in direct relation to the major spaces where the public could find its bearings. Our idea of the museum in this respect is that it is a place where the public must be free to choose its itinerary by knowing its whereabouts and knowing which direction it may take.

Museums and physical disabilities

The Gare d'Orsay, including the portions in stone or plasterwork, had been entirely built on a steel frame. The station was put up only in 1900; it was therefore only eighty years old when we began the work, but whereas the steel frame was intact the glass and plaster had suffered deterioration. There existed a glass-lined passage which we were able to restore without creating safety problems for the visitors.

So as to make the building not only more accessible but also more inviting we built a raised pavement with a colonnade along the Rue de Lille on the same level as the Seine embankment, whereas the street itself is about 1.8 metres lower. We preferred to have a raised base on two sides of the museum with access at several points and with the further advantage of enabling visitors to familiarize themselves with the building by walking along its two sides.

Visitors who enter via the glass-roofed porch on the Rue de Bellechasse will pass through one of the two entrances leading on either side to the information and reception areas. Then comes a row of columns, beyond which are two lifts linking this portion of the building to the various other levels. There is a further lift between the Salle des Fêtes and the embankment entrance, and there are three further ones in other parts of the building.

Naturally the lifts are not the central features dominating the whole design. Its basic element is the treatment of the great central area, the 'promenade', with its three ramps. We start our visit by going down to the former level of the railway lines and then gradually walk up to ground level. The space as a whole is divided up by two lateral ramps and a central one rising successively to different levels; the visitor has the impression of remaining on the ground floor, but in actual fact two levels of the museum are involved, or a little over 7,000 square metres – nearly half the museum space accessible to the public. On the first floor there is an open gallery surrounding the central ground-floor area, and this raises a number of accessibility problems.

For each group of works there is a series of galleries of appropriate proportions, and the layout is fairly easy to grasp, since the central axes running through them in a crosswise direction correspond to the station arches.

The Impressionists are on show in the gallery 'on the heights' – 18.5 metres above the level of the embankment – which is built on the attic floor of the building concealing the 'nave' on the river side. It is reached by lift.

Walking sticks and wheelchairs may be had on request from the cloak-room and anyone who is tired may borrow a wheelchair for the visit. I personally visited the place this way, asking a number of questions in order to test the way things were working and see what still needed adapting. Everything is not ideal and a certain number of things need improving. I would point out that the museum was designed in the late 1970s and early 1980s, i.e. at the moment when the regulations governing accessibility were just coming into force.

The alterations made in front of the main entrance have made the place accessible from the Rue de Lille and from the space in front of the Musée de la Légion d'Honneur down to the embankment, with steps rising very gently. There is also a pavement-level entrance on the embankment side.

There are three ways for disabled people to arrange to visit the museum. There are, first of all, those who come in groups; they will have made an appointment and will be accompanied, and the lift problem will have been fairly easily circumvented, since they will use the goods lifts which can accommodate fairly large groups and do not have the double doors which are the main source of problems. Then there are the people who have made an appointment and can therefore ask to be accompanied during their visit. Lastly, there are those – about fifteen a day – who come by themselves without making an appointment. These are the ones I was mainly interested in.

At the reception desks one may obtain a folder containing a short guide to the areas to be visited and indicating the available lifts. One emerges from the cloakroom into the critical area where one must find one's way to a lift. There are three lifts in the reception area, and a pictogram for the guidance of disabled people. It is here that the problem of the double doors arises. One of the main lifts in the reception area travels down to the former level of the railway lines – 3.6 metres below ground level – where the visit starts. At a still lower level one enters the auditorium, the back rows in which are accessible to disabled people.

All these parts of the building may be entered without a ticket. When the museum was designed considerable importance was attached to the idea of providing a public area of this kind where people could enjoy strolling about.

The visitor next arrives at the point where tickets must be shown, and may then proceed up the slopes in the central area. At the extreme end a lift will provide access to the Impressionist gallery. Here there is first of all a safety door to be opened, and it is fairly heavy. If one wishes to stop at the first floor there will again be a second door when one leaves the lift, and this is the one which creates the most difficulties as the space between the two doors is rather narrow and this one, with its stone facing, is particularly heavy. We know today that all these doors can be machine-operated with the aid of systems which are not excessively expensive considering the size of the building and which would greatly simplify matters. As things are, a person with a walking handicap is obliged to lean on something for support and then pull hard on the door; it will close again fairly rapidly, since it is worked by an automatic device. Hence it is the access to this first floor, where there is the open gallery and where the Rodins are on view, which is at present particularly difficult for the disabled. The upper level, with the gallery 'on the heights', can be reached with little difficulty. The canvases and other exhibits are at suitable height to be easily viewed.

On reaching the end of this gallery one is faced with the dilemma of either going down or else going up to the reference section above the rooftop café. Here again, there is a door shutting off the entry to the lift: we are once more up against the difficulty deriving from the fire-precaution regulations.

A slope leads up to the section devoted to the beginnings of Fauvism, with Matisse and Munch; but first of all there is another lift with a heavy door. This access is in fact very little used because the door is so difficult to open. It would suffice to give it a powered opening device.

I am sorry that at the time of building these several obstructions were not sufficiently considered. I naturally hope everything will be done to turn the museum genuinely into a favourite one for every sort of public.

The 'Venice for all' project, Italy

Piero Cosulich

I shall examine the problem of the accessibility of Venice, a town almost unique in the world and unquestionably a museum town.

The topography of Venice – with its 118 islands separated by 160 canals and linked by 411 bridges – provides a most exciting subject for a study in the abolition of architectural barriers.

We know that none of the islands presents obstacles for disabled persons at ground level, and we find that, with the aid of private or public transport, particularly the *vaporetti*, they may easily travel to and from a great many of them. It should be stressed here that the *vaporetto*, or steamer, is an absolutely suitable and accessible means of transport, whereas the *motoscafo*, or motorboat, is extremely dangerous for the disabled passenger.

A study of a map of the town and of the possibilities afforded by the *vaporetti* will show that 42 per cent of the public buildings of cultural or sightseeing value, and especially the most important administrative buildings admitting the public, are on islands which are not accessible.

The first phase of the proposed project consists in the publication of a map and guide to Venice showing the islands which are accessible. Those which are difficult to access because they may be reached only by *motoscafo* are also shown, as are those not accessible at all on which stand important public buildings or buildings of outstanding interest to the tourist.

In view of the annual influx of tourists, particulars are given of the available accommodation (hotels, boarding houses and rooms to let) on each of the islands shown, and pride of place is given to accommodation which fulfils the basic requirement of being accessible to wheelchairs and which is otherwise most well adapted to the needs of the disabled.

Museums and physical disabilities

It must not be forgotten that today 30 per cent of the Venetian population is elderly; a census taken in 1981 showed that there were 32,000 members of the population over sixty. We may add to these the people suffering from locomotory or sensory disabilities, the children under five, pregnant women and victims of accidents.

We may deduce that, over and above the actually disabled people, who are the most directly affected, 40 per cent of the Venetian population daily comes up against architectural barriers. This proportion is so large that it is not permissible to postpone a thorough examination of the situation any longer. The problem of the accessibility of Venice and of the practicability of its thoroughfares must therefore be tackled and solved in a rational and up-to-date manner, without any sacrifice of Venetian culture and civilization.

The research done on the subject at the University Institute of Architecture by Professor Enzo Cucciniello and his colleagues has produced a professional definition of the priority islands, as a prelude to a start on the work. Venice can become accessible and its thoroughfares practicable once the priority islands not served by water transport have been connected with the neighbouring ones already accessible by *vaporetto*.

Such liaison between the islands is feasible with the aid of a horizontal steel structure described as a 'telescopic mobile footbridge'. Depending on its location, such a bridge may be designed in two different ways, either on a telescopic principle or as a system with a mobile arm. It will be worked by a magnetic card which any disabled or invalid person may obtain from the authorities on application. When introduced into the decoder on the column installed for the purpose this card will produce a series of warning lights and sound signals announcing that the bridge is to move into position. Once the bridge is ready for use it will be accessible via a small automatically worked gate which will close again immediately after the user has passed through it. To fold the bridge back once more the card must be inserted into the decoder on the exit column.

The operations planned under the 'Venice for all' project concern seven different canals.

Under Article 3 of the statute dated 30 April 1985, entitled 'Rules governing the abolition of architectural barriers', the authorities of the Veneto Region have provided for a fund for the execution of the footbridges (as an experiment in infrastructure). The first of the mobile footbridges of the telescopic kind is at present being made; it will give access to the island where the geriatric hospital stands.

The 'Venice for all' project is to be illustrated by a whole series of detailed maps showing the town's most outstanding historic buildings. These are to be clearly shown, with plan view, cross-section and perspective view, on a model in relief accompanied by a description written in braille.

2   At the Greater Louvre a central lift within the spiral staircase enhances the architectural space and ensures access by the main entrance to all visitors.
(Photo: Pierre Michaud)

3   (*opposite*) The majority of disabled people are not in wheelchairs but respect of norms for accessibility is nevertheless essential.
(Photo: Pierre Michaud)

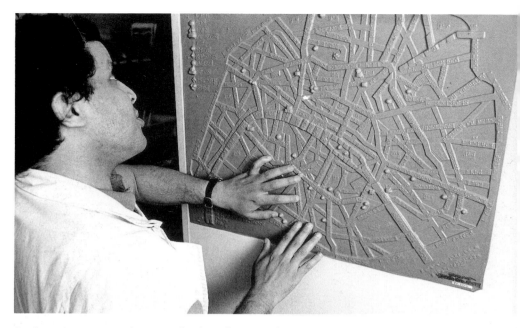

4　Access to museums begins with adapted means of transportation.
(Photo: Pierre Michaud)

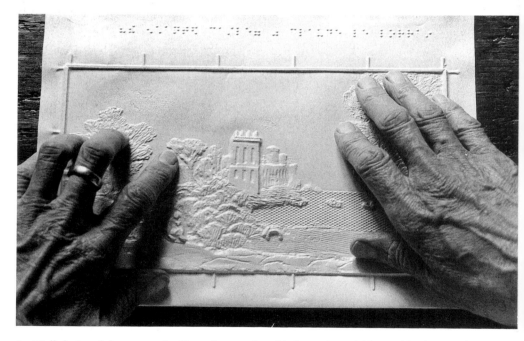

5　Well-designed documents facilitate the transfer of information which would otherwise be inaccessible.
(Photo: Steve Coward. National Gallery, London)

6 Contrasts in line, shape and colour, bold silhouettes are perceptible to 'blind' people with varying forms of residual vision. 'Femme et enfant' by Fernand Léger, 1950.
(Private collection, Paris; © DACS 1991)

7   Religious art and architecture occupy an important place in our culture, and should be made accessible to all.
(Photo: Thierry Le Bow. Association Valentin Haüy)

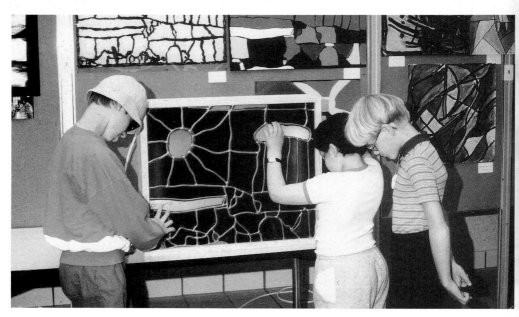

8   For the visually disabled, the study of architecture and cathedrals in particular, can even lead to an understanding of the art of stained glass.
(Photo: *Courrier de l'Ouest*)

9 Carefully selected specimens may be taken out of their showcases for touch sessions.
(Photo: Musée d'histoire naturelle, Bordeaux)

Museums and the visually handicapped

Marcus Weisen

This is one of the very few international series of articles published since 1981 on the subject of museums and the visually handicapped. The Decade of Disabled Persons has come to an end without bringing full awareness to the international community and its member states of the nature of the issues raised by accessibility to museums and to the cultural heritage in general, or of the complexity of the strategies which have yet to be devised if a satisfactory solution to the whole problem is ultimately to be found. A tribute must therefore be paid to the Fondation de France, which has taken the initiative of breaking out of the confines set by national frontiers in order to stimulate a new international dynamic.

Approximately one member in ten of the population of the European countries has a disability. The barriers precluding physical, sensory and educational access to cultural and recreational institutions seriously affect the quality of life of the men and women concerned and that of their families and friends; the problem is *global* in scope and there is no doubt whatsoever that to differing degrees half the population is involved.

The visually handicapped represent 2–3 per cent of the total population of the European Community. Small minorities among these (respectively about 30,000 and about 20,000 in the United Kingdom) are totally blind or are below the school-leaving age. Two-thirds are above retiring age and have thus had a long time in which to grow familiar with their visual sense and visual memory. Among this sector of the population the range of differing types of experience and of perception is extremely wide, and needs are often of a strictly individual nature.

Traditionally the cultural expectations of the low-sighted have always been brushed aside ('You are blind, so you will be unable to paint or carve, and museums are not for you'). We are only just emerging from over a century of the kind of philanthropy which still thoroughly permeates the popular attitude and which we have all inherited; notwithstanding the good intentions it has perhaps led more often to dependency than to freedom for the disabled people concerned. We have yet to provide these people with the necessary means for their self-determination.

In this respect if we are to achieve accessibility to cultural and recreational institutions we must first use our brains on the subtle and complex conditions under which freedom may be experienced and we must actively seek sustenance in the democratic values of the west, abandoning a Eurocentrism which practises discrimination within those very frontiers in which it took shape. The challenge is a gigantic one, for it does not boil down to the preparation of practical programmes, but demands breaks with attitudinal behaviour and changes in such behaviour. Every challenge affords an opportunity for change.

Conditions vary from one country to another and one can only express the desire to see the richer countries devise solutions commensurate with their effective financial possibilities, while intensifying their co-operation with those which are less fortunate.

The present section on museums and the visually handicapped contains a large amount of closely packed reading matter, here and there a little repetitive but bursting with creativeness and inspiration, though reflecting a practical knowledge based on only a few years' experience and as yet incomplete. What we have here is a thin and fragile layer of leaf mould resting on the cultural layers corresponding to some six to ten thousand years of human civilization. What primarily emerges from this wealth of individual contributions is an enthusiasm and a determination to put an end, if only within the framework of an organization, to the barriers to physical, sensory and educational access. But the last word on the subject is not said. At best the contributors propose no more than rough drafts for a global approach. Most of their contributions deal with initiatives exclusively intended for those whose disability is a visual one. In many instances it is a matter of arrangements made specially so as to provide for the wishes and requirements of given individuals or groups and affording optimum conditions of access to the cultural heritage for these. But in so far as there is almost total absence of any prospect of experiences to be enjoyed *independently* (i.e. outside the programme of specially organized visits) and *in the same way as everyone else*, the segregation involved will merely mask the reality of the social segregation that exists. The problem will be solved only when the two approaches are made complementary and when their respective potentials are thus mutually reinforced.

The contributors to this section on museums and the visually handicapped do not propose easy ways of carrying out the job. They oblige readers to use their intelligence; they will discover a whole new series of problems which need to be assimilated. This is at once the strength and the weakness of this approach. Its weakness is a reflection of the pioneer character of an initiative which is all to the credit of those who launched it. It is also a striking reflection of the limited nature of the means of action available to the non-profit-making organizations which have committed themselves to serving the cause of accessibility to cultural institutions.

It is in realization of such weakness that a voice is being raised which, politely but insistently, is demanding the establishment of effective accessibility policies on local, regional and national scales. It is demanding that individual voluntarist action be superseded by *global* action on a political and community level or be subsumed within the latter. It is uttering a major challenge to which any healthy democracy must be able to reply – a challenge to embark on a vast creative and cultural operation which will lay the foundations for authentic cultural integration for the visually handicapped and for all disabled people.

What are involved are freedom, independence and permanency. If the cultural organizations and political institutions do not take charge of launching this huge operation, the achievement of our goal will go the way of all the famous lost causes. But what will be the cost in human terms?

The many forms of visual handicap

Robert Benoist

There are many degrees of visual handicap, ranging from blindness at birth to mild amblyopia or vision little different from the normal. Such handicaps have many different causes and are the consequence of a variety of malformations or diseases. Since I am not an oculist, rather than stressing the medical aspect of the question I will speak of visual handicaps as encountered in everyday life.

The relations entertained by the visually handicapped with museums are only one aspect of a wider problem – that of the relations between these people and their environment. In this respect an initial distinction must be made: the blind and the amblyopic or very low-sighted must be treated as two distinct categories.

Under French law a person is considered to be blind if neither eye with the help of glasses has a central vision equal to or above one-twentieth. The measurement of acuity of vision in tenths is based on the method adopted by eye specialists which consists in assessment of the patient's ability to read letters of a given size at a given distance. Anyone who has been in an oculist's consulting room or in an optician's shop will certainly have seen the boards used for the purpose.

There are no official statistics on the number of blind, but it is generally considered that in France, as in other countries with the same or similar types of civilization and economy, there is one blind person per thousand members of the population and, contrary to what might be imagined, the proportion is not decreasing. While the number of those blind from birth is tending to fall with the progress of obstetrics, the elderly blind are becoming more and more numerous because people now live longer.

The relations of the non-sighted with the outside world will vary according to whether they were blind from birth or have become so later in life after possessing more or less normal vision for a longer or shorter period.

The former category will never have seen at all and will possess no basis of reference enabling them to interpret the explanations they are given in terms of forms, volumes or colours; they will be acquainted with forms and volumes only through touching or holding; as for the word 'colour', it will be meaningless. The other category, on the contrary, will have known volumes and colours in the past and will attach great importance to the intellectual content of the explanations given to them, which will enable them to make use of their recollections. One of my friends, who had become blind in adult life, told me that very often he found an intelligent lecture more worth while than touch exploration.

It may also be noted, again in connection with the differences between those who are born blind and those who become blind later in life, that the former will very early on have acquired a number of useful habits and will have far more efficient substitute senses than the latter, and especially than those who have lost their sight only towards the end of their lives.

No one is ignorant of the importance of what has been acquired in very early youth. Hence it is not surprising that anyone who in childhood became accustomed to feeling, listening and smelling will possess a very special subtlety in the use of the corresponding senses. A blind man who had been blind since early youth recently explained to me that when he had visited a world-famous historic building the sounds and echoes and the vibration of the air had enabled him to grasp the size of the rooms and that the explanations provided in the course of the visit had been far more enjoyable than they would have been if heard elsewhere.

These factors have an important effect on the cultural lives of the two categories. A person born blind will generally read braille fluently, and it may be asserted that for such a person there can be no culture without proficiency in braille. Recently I heard a lecture given by a man born blind who is today reading for an advanced law exam. While he was speaking his fingers ran over his notes as fast as would the eyes of a sighted person reading his text; for his hearers there was no noticeable difference. But people becoming blind late in life will on the contrary have a far less assured touch and will have far greater difficulty in writing, or in reading braille; the later in life they become blind the harder it will be for them to identify the signs. In most cases they will rely entirely on cassettes for access to culture.

Hence when one is planning to present museum exhibits to blind people one must make full allowance for these individual particularities, both in determining the nature and size of the objects to be exhibited and in

Museums and people with impaired vision

The Valentin Haüy Association

The Valentin Haüy Association is an old lady, but it still has a lot of projects. It is a hundred years old, and has always remained faithful to the ideas of its founder, Maurice de La Sizeranne, whose ambition it was to secure co-operation between blind people acquainted with the needs to be met and sighted people who, possessing precisely the competence and the connections which the non-sighted lacked, were in a position successfully to carry through the operations suggested by the latter. A provision which our founder wished to be included in our constitution bears witness to this desire for co-operation, for it makes it compulsory for the Board of Governors to be composed of non-sighted and sighted people in equal numbers. I will add that, likewise under the constitution, the Board must have seven women members. This latter clause, laid down in 1889, denotes on the part of Maurice de La Sizeranne a mentality singularly ahead of its time.

The successive officers of the Association have always sought to preserve this advance, on the principle that nothing of use to the blind could be indifferent to them. For example, those who are in charge of the Association today are keeping close track of the progress of the possibilities afforded by data-processing and electronics for giving the visually handicapped increased independence, or opening up new job opportunities for them.

Since its foundation the Valentin Haüy Association, with its headquarters in Paris and its eighty-one regional or local branches, has been active in two areas, welfare and culture.

Welfare activity covers, among others things, the provision of information to the blind and their families, the hearing of their problems, the granting of loans or subsidies and the running of two remedial employment centres, an institution for school-age children requiring medical supervision, a vocational training-centre, a shop specializing in articles of use to the blind and classes in braille and in getting about without a guide. There are plans for a hostel in Paris and for substantially expanding our remedial work centre near London.

In the cultural sphere our essential role is to print and circulate works in braille and to make and circulate recordings. This year our highly computerized braille printing presses will be bringing out over six million pages. A braille library, the wealthy possessor of 250,000 volumes, lends over 90,000 books per year free of charge, and of our 30,000 musical scores 2,000 were loaned out in 1987. There is also a cassette library containing 4,500 recorded works, and 500,000 cassettes were lent free of charge that same year.

I must further mention the little museum on our premises in the Rue Duroc, which has several exceptionally interesting exhibits illustrating the progress of aids designed to help the blind overcome their handicap, and also a section illustrating the earlier research which preceded the invention of braille. There are a number of sculptures by blind people which have a genuine artistic value.

To conclude this account I will mention the social club created a dozen years ago, which lies at the crossroads of our two sectors of activity, being at once a welfare and a cultural institution. It has organized museum visits ever since it came into existence, initially one a year, then two a year, and finally four in 1988. Their increased frequency is to be explained by the constant demand on the part of the visually handicapped members of the club.

Thus the research undertaken by the Direction des Musées de France for the purpose of enabling the blind and the visually handicapped to derive enjoyment from its many splendid collections is directly in line with what we ourselves are seeking to do, and is the object of a lively interest on our part. We particularly welcomed the co-operation established, through Mr Erlande-Brandenburg, Deputy-Director of French Museums, between the representatives of the Direction and ourselves in connection with the holding of a competition for inventors of facilities or methods enabling blind people to derive greater advantage from their museum visits. We would also pay a tribute to the Fondation de France, which, both in organizing this symposium and in taking part in the aforesaid competition, is testifying to the importance it attaches to the question. And lastly I cannot omit mention of the assistance given by our branch in Blois to the operation carried out at the château by the curator, Ms Tissier de Mallerais.

I would like to end with a few remarks on what we have learned from the twenty or so visits organized since 1977 under the patronage of our Association. I do not mean in so doing to offer advice to the specialists in museography, which would be presumptuous on my part; I merely wish, after describing the conditions under which these visits took place, to tell you of the reactions of the blind or visually handicapped visitors.

The groups are composed of twenty to thirty visually handicapped people accompanied by one sighted person for every four or five of their members. There is always a guide-lecturer who both describes each place or exhibit and places it in its historical or artistic context.

Museums and people with impaired vision

The choice of museum is determined by the possibility or otherwise of touching the exhibits. The first visit was to the Musée Rodin, where the bronzes could be touched by the blind and amblyopic. Subsequently the visitors were given mock-ups, copies or thermoform casts, according to circumstances, or else they were given further access to the original itself. The visitors unquestionably preferred this last alternative, which enabled them to discover what the material used was like. The film made at the Musée de Cluny clearly shows the interest with which the blind visitors ran their hands over fragments of stained glass, discovering in so doing the feel of the polished surface and of the joins between the different small panes. The blind visitors also explored with the greatest interest the forms of the recumbent figures in the Abbey Church of St Denis and the materials of which they were made.

A quite recent visit to a museum in the Marais district which contains a large collection of old locks had significant consequences and I feel it will be worth while pausing a moment to take a look at the way it was conducted and at the sequel it produced. The curator began by bringing together the twenty-five visitors and giving them a talk on the early history of the lock and its mechanisms and on developments in its manufacture over the centuries. To illustrate his remarks he handed round locks fitting the description he gave. The blind and amblyopic visitors were able to hold these in their hands for a considerable time and to examine them from all points of view – their shapes, their mechanisms and the quality of the metal used. They were then taken round the showcases and given further information and further locks to handle. The remarkable fact that should be noted is that subsequently a dozen blind members of the group came back individually for a further visit, thus clearly demonstrating how greatly interested they had been on their first encounter. I recently witnessed a visit to a museum housed in a château where I was struck by the pertinent and interesting nature of the questions asked. In general all the visits have aroused a lively interest among those who have taken part and from remarks subsequently heard it may be legitimately deduced that they have unquestionably been a great success.

It is not for me to draw practical conclusions concerning the organization of museums from the few practical points to which I have referred. But I trust my remarks will give food for thought to those whose intention it is to enable the blind to share in the aesthetic pleasure afforded by museums and historic buildings to those who are privileged to possess two eyes perfectly fulfilling their function.

An introduction to art as a means to a therapy to be practised by disabled and non-sighted people

Michel Bourgeois-Lechartier

It is widely felt that the greatest service we can render the disabled and the blind is to give them as far as possible the means of being like anyone else. Is it not curious that in so many ancient civilizations the blind man should have been imagined to see more clearly than the sighted – so much so that Oedipus finally puts out his eyes in order to see, while blind old Tiresias has seen what Oedipus failed to perceive when his eyes were open?

Our eyes are often as objective as a camera lens and as capable of providing us with a faithful analysis. But is vision no more than the product of an optical mechanism? Does not the artist, whether writer, musician, painter, sculptor or architect, seek through methodical obser-vation of reality to give life to a vision which goes far beyond that reality and beyond his own horizon?

When we gaze for a long time at an orange-red fabric brilliantly lit up against a white background, most of us perceive that it gives off a magnificent blue-green radiance. Very frequently – and I have had repeated proof of this – the handicapped see this radiance immediately and even almost exclusively; it arrests their gaze and they remain lost in motionless contemplation, so dazzled as to have lost interest in all else. In actual fact what we have is a perfectly natural and automatic optical phenomenon; each colour radiates its complementary colour; it is merely a matter of reverberation of light on a coloured object. But the Asian world has taught us that radiances, as they grow increasingly subtle, condense themselves into an 'aura'. We must therefore realize that a great many disabled people, as their paintings frequently show, see us essentially through an 'aura' of the sort. Even a blind person will perceive us in this way, though doubtless here it will be a question of atmosphere rather than of light. Of this we cannot have a precise idea – any more than, in many cases, may he or she.

However, this initial discovery of the radiance given off by so unimportant a thing as a piece of cloth must help us make a complete change in our approach to the disabled. Our words and our gestures have no meaning for them if they do not correspond to our psychological 'radiance' and thus reflect our inner truth. It is for this reason that any behaviour contrary to the promptings of our innermost feelings will cause disabled people to withdraw into solitude in order to escape the polluted atmosphere created for them by the impression that our apparent good will is no more than a disguise. In contrast, they will often be more sensitive than we are to a work of art where there is total harmony between the artist's vision and the ultimate significance of what the work represents.

This raises the question of our way of seeing shapes: a round collar will give the lower part of the face a rounded form, whereas an open and pointed collar will give the chin a more angular look. Similarly the colour of the eyes will alter with that of the scarf framing the face.

Our eyes are so used to seeing without taking the trouble to look that the gaze of the artist is as alien to us as is that of the disabled person. Both the one and the other feel the rhythm in the lines, the fulness of the volumes and the magic of the colours so much more intensely than we, who most frequently look even at the human being as objectively, as coldly and as mechanically as would a camera lens.

We nowadays recognize the human being with the aid of his identity photograph. There is an anecdote worth quoting here by way of contrast: a Kanaka woman, who is to go and fetch a child and is afraid of not identifying him is told: 'You'll see him straight away: children of chiefs always look different from other children.'

The disabled tend far more than we do to retain the inner life of children. If we say to a little girl: 'Go and play with your doll' our language will create a barrier and the child will withdraw, for we will have been using the wrong sort of language. If, on the contrary, we tell her: 'Mary is crying, hurry up and comfort her', the child will have listened and it will be not a mere inanimate doll but her daughter Mary whom she will take in her arms.

What matter for us are the concrete actions, but for the disabled material actions will acquire concrete reality only if the heart goes along with them; otherwise their minds will be elsewhere even while they perform them.

If we are to understand a disabled person's reactions to ourselves and to works of art, we must also remember how often the face can lie. How many people whom we dislike do we greet with smiles! The eyes of a child who is telling a lie will open wide to give the appearance of speaking the truth . . .

It is for this reason that the visually handicapped may be more readily likened to the artist who prefers to interpret and express the human heart through the attitude of the body, which will often be truer than the facial expression. The drooping shoulders of someone dear to us will tell us of that person's weariness, and the airy steps of a little girl will keep time to her inner song and dance. This was clear to Rodin, and explains the expressiveness of his sculptures. We find the same knowledge in Michelangelo, Dürer, Goya and others. Similarly, Ukyo-e prints emphasize the forcefulness of the attitudes expressed by a brush-stroke.

The non-sighted person is not merely unable to see the bodies of other people, but will even have difficulty in sensing how his or her own body fits into space. Furthermore, there is no recourse to a mirror for a non-sighted person. We ourselves feel the backs of our necks only if we have a headache. A healthy body remains forgotten, unless a clumsy dancer steps on our toes. The non-sighted person will not feel his or her body any more than we do; but that body will be rudely awakened every time it receives a knock from an object standing in its way. Non-sighted people will thus prefer to avoid such risks by restricting their activities. We do not generally notice that we have scratched a spot, but our mirror will duly point this out. The non-sighted will often learn of such a fact through an unpleasant remark, for example: 'How ugly you look with that spot!' A little blind girl will so often have been told, when wearing a frock: 'Put your legs together, we can see your knickers' that she will not dare to spread her knees even when wearing trousers. For the non-sighted we are as gods, able to know things about themselves of which they themselves are not even aware, such as scratching themselves or putting their fingers up their nose. Yet the body will lose its vitality if it stiffens into an attitude beyond all criticism.

This should be enough to convince us of the need to provoke the non-sighted into arousing their own physical sensations. The youth who remarked 'I always used to be cold before' was at last rediscovering his body. Encasing oneself in imaginary armour or failing to control one's gestures may represent the vengeance of a body too long forgotten and may remain necessities for a certain length of time. The blind child, even more than the sighted one will need not only the experience of fighting, sport or a warm shower but also his father's knees, his mother's fondlings, the calm and the understanding of his grandparents or the arm of a friend. The inner vision of works of art as developed in the non-sighted person by the practice of this method calls for a body as palpably present to its

adopting key attitudes as a means of altering his mood and had achieved genuine self-control, in absolute contrast to the impression of power-lessness which had previously dominated his make-up. 'Hurry up,' some of them will urge, 'and show us the key attitudes to use.' These, unfor-tunately, do not exist, for no attitude is devoid of danger.

Certain attitudes, if lived intensely, produce unbearable wants and urges related to personal problems, and it is far from easy for the outsider to help to overcome these. There is a ninth-century Sanskrit poem which perhaps answers the question:

> While her husband was feigning sleep at her side, the young bride laid
> her cheek on his cheek, with great difficulty refraining from the joy of
> a passionate kiss. He in his turn refrained from making the slightest
> gesture, for fear that she might draw back through modesty. And so
> the two of them, refraining from doing what they so intensely
> desired, felt their hearts transported beyond the utmost peak of desire.

If a woman or a girl is made to stand as though holding a baby, an attitude which is one of the most self-fulfilling for either, the sensation of the baby's presence (although there is in reality no baby) will generally produce magnificent smiles. But if the woman involved has seen a child run over in the street, or has had an abortion, or if her baby is at home ill, there is a likelihood that she will be plunged into a state of deep affliction. A woman may feel herself, intellectually and morally, to be perfectly 'liberated' and may choose abortion with no qualms whatsoever. But if, at some deeper level, she has preserved a feeling of guilt, the experience born of the sensation of holding a baby may lead to inner 'destructuralization'. It must be emphasized that although there is no baby, or doll, or any sort of substitute, I am very often told: 'It's strange, I've often held a baby and I've never felt its presence so intensely or loved it so much.'

Where there is total physical relaxation and total mental and emotional absence of commitment, the inner experience is felt infinitely more deeply and authentically than would be the case in real circumstances. Perhaps Plato's myth of the underground cave is not merely a myth?

There are therefore real dangers. There is first of all the risk of reliving, with an utter absorption of one's entire being, a trial which one had imagined to be over and done with; but there is also the risk that figments of the imagination may become objects of live experience and be lived through with an acuity particularly dangerous because all levels of the being will be involved, even if this is only faintly realized.

Art as therapy for disabled and non-sighted people

In the Aphorisms of Patanjali we read: 'When there is cessation of all the movements of thought and of the impressions of the subconscious mind, the spirit resembles the purest crystal; subject, object and instrument of knowledge coincide and there is unification.' We find the same idea in the Cabbala: 'Something will be renewed and "engendered" each time there is convergence between thinker, thought and the object of the thought.'

'In reality,' says Mircea Eliade, 'if there exists complete solidarity among the human race, it can be felt and "actuated" only on the level of images (we will not say "of the subconscious" since there is nothing to prove that there is not also a transconscious).' Here the word 'image' naturally means more than 'work of art', since the work of art is no more than the reflection or image of deeper realities. 'The symbol, the myth, and the image belong to the substance of spiritual life. They may be camouflaged, mutilated or degraded, but will never be totally uprooted.'

It is because it touches the most deep-seated level of our being that the aforementioned method presents dangers. Our own discovery of the work of art generally lies at a shallower level than the discovery thus afforded to the blind or disabled. Very often we 'judge' the plastic merits of a work from the outside, with the detachment of the critic, instead of following the great tradition of contemplation which leads to identification with the work.

If we think about the initial use made of what we now call a work of art we will find our present conception to be absolutely mistaken. When Egypt was peopled by innumerable statues representing Pharaoh, was the intention not to make his fearful yet benevolent presence felt extensively among the population? When in Africa, Asia or Oceania men put on the sacred mask, did they not become a part of forces mightier than themselves? When the believer places a candle in front of a statue or icon, is his prayer not a direct conversation, not with the stone or wood, but with the spiritual presence invoked by means of it? When a child stands open-mouthed and with wide eyes staring at a picture of motherhood does it not inwardly become the baby lovingly enwrapped in its mother's arms? In short, does not any contemplation of a work of art and any participation in it initially derive from identification with it?

Here lies the explanation for the self-curative function of such initiation into art. Either the conscious mind finds in the painted or carved 'image' the reflection of its own sources of happiness and blossoms out, or else it sees in it a picture of its own affliction, which it is thus enabled to control or sublimate. A balanced sequence of attitudes typically expressive of the feelings of the human being will make possible a progress from psychological disturbance to mastery of the subject's inner life. This explains why for purposes of a programme of initiation into art the instructor will take his or her inspiration not from the works in fashion or on the contemporary market but from the universally acclaimed masterpieces in which artists have best succeeded in expressing both their imaginary universe and their discovery of a beauty filling their hearts with peace and plenitude. Art, from the witches of Goya to the women of Botticelli or Renoir, from Rodin's *Burghers of Calais* to the work of Mykerinos, from *Guernica* to representations of motherhood by Picasso or Rouault, the *Death of Sardanapale* or the *Raft of the 'Medusa'* to the *Virgin at the Foot of the Cross*, is certainly the language most expressive of the human emotions.

Whereas we will frequently be satisfied with observing but not embracing the feelings expressed, the non-sighted will experience them inwardly. Let us not forget that when we, the sighted, look at an exhibition in a museum, our eyes automatically turn aside from anything we dislike and attach themselves on the contrary to whatever suits our own sensibility. The non-sighted, on the contrary, cannot choose what they are to look at; they will be acquainted with the work only once they have experienced it within themselves. Only then will they know whether they like it or whether it disgusts them. Instructors must therefore be in such close communion with the person undergoing the experience that they will be able to give a positive turn to something that was in danger of becoming harmful.

You will now understand why the instructors need a two-year training.

The method has, in effect, necessitated long years of research into dreams, the imagination and the different levels of consciousness. But it has finally taken shape as a result of a comparative study of religions and of traditional approaches to visions and to ecstasy, with necessary rejection of any use of drugs or forms of hypnosis which would result in loss of consciousness and so restrict the blind person's freedom of choice. For the tie-up between the physical and the psychological, the meridians and points for acupuncture are exploited in accordance with the instructor's different tactile techniques, particularly the Shiatsu technique.

Naturally what succeeds in the case of those blind from birth also succeeds for both the physically and the mentally handicapped, as it succeeds of course with so-called 'normal' people. Schoolchildren, in particular, are most receptive to so unusual a way of exploring art.

The blind and museums: choosing works of art for tactile observation

Gilles Grandjean

The diversity of museum publics is such that museum authorities have found themselves having to think hard about the ways of satisfying them all. There are the demands which are more readily catered for in that they stem from those groups which are constantly growing in size – young people, for example. But there are also more restricted groups equally anxious to be listened to and anxious in their turn to gain admittance to a heritage which they consider belongs to them as well: I refer here to the disabled. Of these the blind and the visually handicapped raise a specific problem of approach to works of art – the approach through tactile exploration.

The golden rule in a well-kept museum is PLEASE DO NOT TOUCH. How can this rule be relaxed without harmful effects on the conservation of the exhibits?

As a point of departure for an initial attempt to reply to this question we may take the various events and experiments arranged by the Cultural Activities Department of the Direction des Musées de France between 1982 and 1987. The exhibitions entitled 'Human Faces', 'Romanesque Capitals' and '19th-century French Sculpture' were, in effect, revealing as illustrations of the changing attitude of curators towards the accessibility of the works displayed to tactile exploration.

The earliest of these, 'Human Faces', held at the former Musée d'Art et d'Essai in Paris, made use of about thirty casts as means of telling the history of the portrayal of the human face from the earliest times to our own day by a number of different civilizations. It is only fair to point out that the idea of this initiative grew out of the various exhibitions made available to the public by the Musées Royaux d'Art et d'Histoire in Brussels. Though it met with widespread success it also aroused criticism, not to say disappointment, in various quarters – a reflection of the feeling of frustration experienced by a great many visitors at not being presented with originals.

In view of these criticisms it was decided to make an improvement in the system when, in 1983, the 'Romanesque Capitals' exhibition, held once again at the Musée d'Art et d'Essai, was in preparation. This no longer meant organizing a special exhibition for the visually handicapped but devising one to suit all categories of visitors. Casts were used as material for preliminary study preparing the visitor for the exhibition proper, where ten or so actual original works could be felt with the hands. Hence the casts section merely provided a basis for reference or comparison with regard to form or style, using extremely well-known masterpieces either not on show in the exhibition or unable to be touched.

It is important to note that casts, though they must not be the curator's excuse for not permitting the touching of originals, are not to be systematically rejected. In the case of essential masterpieces unsuitable for touching but of decisive importance for an understanding of the history of sculpture casts possess the same documentary value as the photographs in an art book. It would be a pity to forgo so irreplaceable an aid to study through excessive anxiety to exhibit nothing but originals. Obviously where possible it is preferable to confine oneself to originals, as was done in 1985 in the very big '19th-century French Sculpture' exhibition at the Grand Palais. In this instance blind visitors were presented with about fifteen works by the greatest masters, illustrating a broad selection of materials and techniques. Thus within only a few years there had been a distinct change in the attitude of the curators; progressively overcoming their fear of seeing originals fingered, and reassured by a growing body of practical experience, they were now making available a progressively widening range of works.

However, the selection of such works calls for extreme vigilance; some of them are too fragile, and in general their degree of 'legibility' for the visually handicapped will tend to vary.

The genius of the sculptor has been served by an infinite variety of materials, from the hardest diorite to the most fragile *papiers collés*. Works of art are above all material things. And materials, far from possessing the apparent stability one would ascribe to them, are on the contrary living substances which develop, undergo change and may also, unfortunately, become diseased.

Laboratory research such as that carried out by the Direction des Musées de France teaches us to become better acquainted with materials and above all compels us to be increasingly circumspect where they are concerned. We now know that climate changes, moisture, salts (perspiration), attack the surfaces of works of art to an infinitesimal and therefore invisible degree. Careless handling can mar the work of the restorers who attempt to halt the ageing process where possible, or at least slow it down.

The purpose of these remarks is to explain the predicament of anyone in charge of a collection who is asked for permission for the works in his care to be touched. Is he to refuse? Naturally not; but the greatest possible circumspection will be called for.

There must first of all be a scrupulous examination of the works in question and dismissal of those which are fragile as a result of restoration, relatively old, or composed of separate parts not too securely assembled (perhaps with arms and legs merely socketed on). There will also be those with veneering or inlaid decoration. Polychrome works and those bearing traces of colour cannot be touched either without risk of deterioration.

Let us now take a look at the main categories of materials from the point of view of their strength or weakness.

Stone, with which we will start, and which is the most usual material for sculpture, may be of very variable degrees of hardness, depending on its texture and on its coherence. Certain limestones and most sedimentary rocks can have scratches left on them by finger-nails and are in any case to be ruled out since they are difficult to polish and often have an unpleasant feel. Marbles, whose hardness varies, will often be sufficiently resistant and will be particularly suitable if they have been polished and are thus scarcely permeable to dirt. Hard stones such as granite, diorite, basalt or porphyry, whose surface is practically unattackable, may be safely touched. This is an admittedly rather simplistic classification; but it tends to show that the works of certain periods or civilizations – those of ancient Egypt or oriental antiquity, for example – which are associated with the use of very hard stones will be easier to present than others, and this does in fact raise problems when programmes for visitors are being worked out.

Apart from the precautions against the risks of breakage, which are very minor if care has been taken to ensure that the works are properly stable, the most important thing is to see that the visitors' hands are clean and dry. This is true in the case of all materials, but is especially so when dealing with stone, particularly stone with a low-density texture which absorbs dirt and moisture. It is easy to provide visitors with paper towels and to request them to wipe their hands frequently. One must also remember to dust the works beforehand so as to avoid finger-marks. A further precaution will be to ask people to remove their rings, as these may leave scratches on soft materials.

Pottery will be liable to the same surface damage as stone and when selecting archaeological finds one must first be sure of their stability in the presence of salt. The main obstacle to the handling of pottery is its fragility.

Metal objects whose surface has become oxidized and is therefore unstable are to be ruled out, as are highly oxidizable metals such as silver. When dealing with bronzes one's choice must be guided by the condition of the patina and its degree of resistance; but after tactile examination a bronze work must always be wiped to preclude oxidation resulting from small deposits of moisture.

Organic materials are certainly the most fragile of all. The only one which may be touched is thoroughly sound wood, and even then veneering and inlay must be ruled out. Ancient fabrics, and ivory, bone, horn and other organic materials will almost always be ineligible for selection owing to their extreme fragility and their excessive sensitivity to moisture. Often the only way of conveying an impression of works made of them will be via the use of casts supplemented by series of samples.

Objective criteria reflecting the imperatives of conservation will thus have led to the making of an initial selection from among the exhibits in the museum. A fresh selection will remain to be made, especially if the works are to illustrate a lecture. This task will be of a far more subjective nature, the aim being to choose the works which are most representative and significant and which are also the most accessible to the visually handi-capped visitor. The tactile exploration of a work – for the process may be rightly termed a voyage of discovery – is a very slow business and visits for the blind last a long time. One cannot therefore afford to let the visitor's attention be diverted to works which are lacking in interest because they are of mediocre value or are very difficult to conceive of as a whole because their composition is confusing. This time the selecting cannot be the responsibility of the curator alone; he or she will need the assistance of blind persons or of representatives of associations able to guide the choice in the light of their experience, especially if they are versed in art.

The fact is that the same object will have at once a visual image and a tactile image and the two may not coincide. For example, if the object one wishes to show is Baroque and is composed of an overabundance of details its tactile effect will be merely one of confusion. If, on the contrary, it is relatively plain it will be possible to render perceptible the play of the curves and counter-curves and to convey one of the features of Baroque. But the museum visit must not consist merely in the exploration of objects treated as purely documentary evidence: the visitor must sense the enjoyment to be derived from any encounter with a work of art. Certain materials, certain surfaces and certain forms are more capable than others of giving this kind of satisfaction. The warmth of wood, the lustrous patina of marble and the perfect smoothness of polished diorite produce sensations particularly pleasant to the touch. The same thing may be said of sizes and shapes. Though it is impossible to present works of monumental size for blind people to acquaint themselves with directly, smaller works whose volume may be readily grasped and whose proportions may be encompassed will afford them a great deal of satisfaction.

Clarity of composition must, furthermore, be one of the priorities when choosing works for tactile examination, especially if the visitors are making their first acquaintance with a museum. A work with an abundance of detail may be shown; but the true nature of the artist's intention will be more readily discerned where the outlines are spare. In animal sculpture, for example, a work in which the animal's coat has been rendered in detail will be far less readily understood than an Egyptian work in which the forms are stylized; the coat so soft to the touch in reality will be totally formless, hard and unwelcome when represented in sculpture.

Details of this kind are actually pictorial additions to the sculptured forms, and certain works of sculpture are transpositions into three-dimensional space of a two-dimensional image. The most obvious illustration of this is provided by those works of sculpture whose composition introduces the notion of perspective and of vanishing point; these are very difficult to render comprehensible to visually handicapped visitors, or at least to newcomers. For just as the eye can be trained to look at art the touch can acquire greater sensitivity, and visitors who have come to the museum several times are more receptive and more sensitive than those who are paying their first visit. Hence the importance of regularly opening our museum galleries to the blind and visually handicapped.

To conclude, and in the hope of opening up prospects which will be an encouragement to us in our desire to make our museums available to an ever-increasing number of visitors, we must stress the fact that the success of the various initiatives will be dependent on the general will to co-operate and on mutual understanding between the different parties concerned.

Above all, the museums must understand the irreplaceable nature of their role and the immense potential source of satisfaction they represent for the disabled. But the latter must also understand the imperatives to which museums are subject and which do not always permit them fully to live up to their aspirations.

The last and most important point is that, as experience has shown, the human qualities of the staff, whether curators, attendants or lecturers, will suffice to smooth out the difficulties inherent in the institutions themselves, since, where given requirements cannot be avoided, a solution will invariably be found, even if only of a makeshift nature and even if valid only in particular circumstances of time and place.

Art and the visual handicap. A role for the associations for the blind, the museums and art associations and the official cultural authorities

Marcus Weisen

My remarks will be based on a simple notion. Disabled people are entitled to the same cultural life as the rest of us and their right to it is inalienable. This right has found its contemporary expression in Article 27.1 of the Universal Declaration of Human Rights, which runs: 'Everyone has the right freely to enjoy the artistic and cultural life of the community.'

Attitudinal obstacles, inadequate adaptation of premises and the difficulty of obtaining reliable and complete information preclude the disabled from access to a vital dimension of contemporary relations with culture: the extensive range of possible choices, the appeal of distant prospects, freedom from any sort of trusteeship and an unending itinerary of places and events to be travelled through.

For the disabled the right freely to enjoy artistic and cultural life has a meaning only if the community frees them from the obstacles to their access to a cultural and creative experience which in other respects is fully within their reach.

This paper will confine itself to the visual arts. I shall attempt in it to measure the impact of the creation of a post of 'arts officer' by a national association, provide a few data permitting an assessment of recent initiatives in the United Kingdom and propose a few conclusions more general in scope.

In June 1987 the Royal National Institute for the Blind (RNIB) set an example to the other big national associations for the disabled by being the first to appoint an arts officer. Its primary objective was to promote the access of visually handicapped people to the world of art and culture, especially to those areas of that world which had long been considered inaccessible or accessible only to a limited degree, namely, museums, the architectural heritage, painting, sculpture, dancing and dramatic art. The initiative was a response to the appeal launched by the Carnegie Council, whose inquiry into 'Arts and Disabled People' (*The Attenborough Report* 1985), had brought to light the endemic inadequacy of the resources provided nationally for the disabled people of Great Britain for integrated activity in the field of art. The creation of the post was an aspect of a wider movement for the defence of the cultural rights of disabled people, the origin of which dates back at least to the creation of Shape (1976) and whose expansion, though it has acquired lightning speed during these past few years, has for the most part failed to penetrate beyond the confines of the official artistic and cultural institutions.

Information always circulates with difficulty inside the world of the visually handicapped. It is not unusual for the latter to be the last to learn of an artistic or museological event intended for their benefit. One of my main official tasks is therefore to produce and circulate such information. The structures for its circulation are extremely complex (230 local or regional associations for the blind, 500 local 'cassette newspapers', a dozen nationwide publications combining braille with cassettes and the printed word, 60 special schools, 60 integrated schools admitting large numbers of visually handicapped pupils in special sections, 600 or so integrated schools admitting visually handicapped pupils, a national radio programme and several regional ones for the visually handicapped and the municipal welfare services). It is thus a matter of patiently making one's presence felt and intensifying that presence by improving the machinery for circulating information and by organizing events which may serve as catalysers of public opinion and the media of publicity.

The other side of my work consists in helping museums, art galleries, theatres, ballet companies and creative workshops to prepare and publicize projects, integrated or otherwise, for the visually handicapped, or else – as is becoming progressively more frequent – putting them in touch with individuals or organizations capable of providing the necessary expert guidance; often the individuals involved here are themselves visually handicapped. The British refer to this as 'networking'.

In 1988 funds allocated to the promotion of the arts, combined with some modest contributions, made possible the implementing of a score of projects on scales ranging from small to medium or large. The official and prompt support of the RNIB – whose name is respected by prospective sponsors – was doubtless instrumental in enabling funds for these projects to be doubled or trebled. (I would not care to see the British system for funding exported abroad. The British cultural authorities have a mercantile approach to art which condemns all pioneers in our field to spend the best part of their time collecting the necessary funds before they can launch any new and necessary project. I trust that within the coming few years the cultural authorities of the countries of Europe will recognize that what is at issue is a human right of which the disabled are deprived and not a luxury which the community can do without.)

Here I will list a series of public events designed to promote knowledge of our subject, namely:

1. 'Talking Touch' (February 1988), a seminar on the use of touch in museums and art galleries, organized jointly with the Museums and Galleries Disability Association (MAGDA). This seminar, attended by 135 people, was the first big national forum for exchanges of information between the museum world, the art world and the associations of visually handicapped persons. The following week a further seminar was held, 'Art and Education for Visually Handicapped People', organized by the Adult Education Department of Leicester University.

2. 'An Eye for Art' (February–July 1988), the first national painting competition for visually handicapped pupils, in which all the schools concerned, whether integrated or not, were invited to take part. Two hundred pupils, from about fifty schools in all, submitted entries, many of which were of a high standard. Two of the four members of the jury – respectively an artist and a theatrical producer – were themselves visually handicapped. The project was designed to fulfil a dual purpose: to render the schools alive to the creative capacities of their blind or visually handicapped pupils and to encourage these pupils' creativeness. A selection of the works submitted was used to illustrate the RNIB's annual calendar for the subsequent year.

This event represented in itself a mild revolution in attitudes within an organization for the blind. Whereas previous RNIB calendars had entitled all their illustrations 'The beauty they can't see', the new one made it clear that it was now a question of 'the beauty they know how to create and see'.

A selection of the paintings was also exhibited for five weeks at the Gunnersbury Park Museum in West London.

A forthcoming competition is to embrace all forms of the visual arts, and in order to avoid penalizing totally blind and very low-sighted pupils, sculpture is to be included. However, the criteria for judging and ability to form a judgement tend to suffer when the works are those of pupils with widely varying types of vision.

3. 'An Eye for Art' (September–October 1988), organized jointly with Gunnersbury Park Museum. This was a national exhibition of paintings and photographs by eight visually handicapped or blind artists; it contained a total of about a hundred works, all of a high standard. Four of

the artists had just completed their course at an art school, two had studied art before their sight had begun to fail and two painters, one of whom was totally blind, were self-taught.

The press had for once been obliged to abandon the outdated clichés on blindness and defective vision and on the whole its assessment was a positive one. Yet the underlying concept on which the exhibition had been based remained ambiguous; all the artists had in common were their visual handicaps, varying in degree of gravity. However, unity was imparted to the whole via a less readily apparent theme, that of the world of perception, and most of the public reacted very favourably to this as a subject for further thought. I would advise anyone interested in this approach to obtain the catalogues of the exhibitions entitled, respectively, 'Art of the Eye: an Exhibition on Vision' published by Forecast, Public Artspace Productions, Minneapolis, USA, 1988–9), and 'Anders Gezien' (Ostend Museum of Modern Art, 1987), both of which were adequately financed and represent in my opinion the most successful initiatives in this area.

4. 'Arts and Crafts' (December 1988), a seminar organized by local and regional associations for the blind and by municipal welfare services. It had the dual purpose of enabling artists and the teachers of arts and crafts employed by a minority of local associations for the blind or by welfare services to escape from their isolation and to illustrate the range of activities which could provide alternatives to basketwork – an occupation frequently decried but perfectly legitimate provided it co-exists with a choice of other arts-and-crafts activities.

5. The initiative taken by *New Beacon* (the RNIB journal), which, alone among specialized periodicals, decided to devote a monthly page to the arts, with a leading article and a diary of events.

To limit the regular circulation of information on art and the visually handicapped to the specialized periodicals was felt to involve the danger of a new sort of 'ghettoization'. For this reason co-operation was established with *Artists' News*, one of the foremost British art journals. At the present time similar co-operation is being established with MAGDA and with the *Museums Journal* with a view to regular publication of information on museums and the disabled. An original approach has been taking shape: information will not necessarily be published in a section entitled 'Museums and Disablement'; frequently it will appear in reports on seminars or on exhibitions or under similar headings.

6. In 1988, the RNIB, in co-operation with the Museums Association Data Base, carried out a survey of 2,400 museums concerning the accessibility of museums and art galleries for the visually handicapped. The

thirty-six questions asked formed a part of the annual questionnaire, to which 1,368 museums or galleries replied. The number of valid answers varied from 1,179 to 1,285 according to the question asked.

The results of the survey were as follows:

69%   of the museums or galleries providing valid answers anticipate making arrangements for visits for the visually handicapped.
46%   allow at least ten objects to be touched.
25%   had arranged 'handling sessions' during the twenty-four preceding months.
 4.5% provide a cassette guide.
4%   provide a large-print guide.
2.5% provide a braille guide.
10%   have large-type labels.
 1%   have braille labels.
55%   would like advice on how to organize handling sessions.
69%   would like advice on how to adapt to the needs of the disabled.

A brief study of the statistics shows that the majority of those museums which allow certain objects on exhibition to be touched do not have adequate guides. In the rare cases where information is available in a form which is accessible to the visually disabled, it is almost always a literal transcription of general information prepared for the sighted public and, as such, remains an abstract, literary experience for the visually handicapped. In the absence of museum guides for the visually handicapped, the latter have no means of knowing what is available for them. And as long as such information is not included in museum guides for the general public, one cannot speak of true cultural integration.

A brief assessment of the situation in the United Kingdom

The visually handicapped are far from having secured artistic and cultural integration. Since 1975 there have been a number of initiatives, most of them the result of individual commitment, which have served to create an atmosphere conducive to a distinct improvement in accessibility to the cultural heritage; since 1987 such initiatives have multiplied to an unprecedented extent, with several dozen projects in all, fifteen or so tactile exhibitions open to everyone and a few operations on a nationwide scale (e.g. 'Cathedrals through Touch and Hearing'). A public dimension and public recognition are little by little being achieved.

The fact that a national association for the blind should have involved itself in the process has acted as a very real catalyser. Information is more readily able to circulate and a new sort of expert knowledge is developing.

Museums and people with impaired vision

The barren age of isolation is gradually being left behind.

On the whole, the recent initiatives have only rarely led to the institution of permanent infrastructures. Only a handful of museums are providing conditions of educational and sensory accessibility which may be exploited autonomously. Museological programmes for the visually handicapped, which originated in the Mary Duke Biddle Gallery for the Blind in North Carolina, USA, in 1963, still remain for the most part confined to touch activities, whereas only 5–10 per cent of the visually handicapped are actually blind. Museum programmes catering partly for those with residual vision remain the exception.

For the museums and their clientele the need for the passing-on of information and for the discovery of new experiences remains enormous, and the task is far beyond the means of associations for the blind. It will involve the creation of new jobs, the provision of funds, a high level of planning and museological proficiency. A noteworthy and lasting improvement in the highest degree can take place only if the authorities and museum associations themselves take an overall initiative in the right direction.

While it is unquestionable that these organizations must accept ever-increasing responsibility, it is equally essential for the associations for the blind to do the same. Nothing but co-operation between these hitherto totally separate worlds and a combination of the unique expert knowledge of each can provide the necessary basis for a fundamental improvement. If the change is to be lasting and to be to the advantage of everyone, it must take place at all levels.

If we except those few museums and art galleries whose tactile exhibitions open to all attract record numbers of visitors, the majority of the initiatives taken in the United Kingdom may be said to survive only with the aid of private donations of a philanthropic nature. From the community point of view such a situation is totally at variance with the dignity attaching to the human and cultural issues bound up with accessibility.

The community cannot but enrich itself by taking vigorous steps to initiate the process of artistic and cultural integration for the disabled; but this is a cause whose pursuit does not require the justification of being in the interests of the community at large. It is first and foremost a matter of an individual right – a right which places binding moral obligations on the community, and consciousness of this fact must transform itself into a genuine political will for change.

If, in the first place, the changes will affect the disabled people themselves, they will also affect their families and friends and the quality of their social life: a good half of the population is involved.

It is time for the authorities to be studying possible legislation governing physical, sensory and educational accessibility to artistic and cultural institutions. The American example shows that anti-discrimination laws are not enough in themselves to solve the problem of accessibility and that for such laws to be operational adequate practical means must be provided.

'Blindness is not a necessity.' In the area we are concerned with these words of William Kirby's excellently summarize the question at issue.

Lateral repercussions

> I cannot restrain myself from touching statues; I turn away my eyes and my hand goes on exploring by itself: neck, head, nape, shoulders ... The sensations come flocking to my finger-tips. No single one of them but is different from the rest, so that my hand travels over a most varied and animated landscape.
>
> Jean Genet, *L'Atelier d'Alberto Giacometti*

Some tens of thousands of British people have visited one or other of the recent tactile exhibitions open to everyone and have been able to share Genet's exultation and his exaltation of the rediscovery of touch as a way of approaching the world. In touching the sculptures their hands have revealed the negative side of the intellectualist rationality of the western world, which ever since the Renaissance has been unilaterally cultivating and overcultivating the visual sense.

Tactile exhibitions open to all are creating a new point of departure for thought on the subject of the so-called 'inferior' senses and the growing interest in art and residual vision is providing food for a broader enquiry into the nature of perception. It might well be that so original a combination may give birth to new artistic and perceptual practices.

The new technologies in the service of visually handicapped visitors to museums

Hoëlle Corvest

The work of the Disablement Committee at the Cité des Sciences et de l'Industrie (CSI) at La Villette (Paris) has placed strong emphasis on the idea that research on accessibility necessarily calls for the active collaboration of disabled people. Intrinsic knowledge acquired by first-hand experience of the realities of everyday life is in effect an incentive to practical analysis of the facts and to the suggesting of solutions which may prove satisfactory. In addition, the presence of official representatives of associations and contacts on practical matters during work or at social events provide a reliable means of instilling the relevant information and doing away with the myth surrounding disablement. Awareness of realities will gradually alter the conventional mental image, which often leads to over-dramatization or underestimation of what is involved.

Thus since September 1986 I have been on the staff of the CSI, where I am responsible for researching into accessibility for the visually handicapped public and putting my findings into practice.

Over and above the practical organization of a range of activities for individuals groups, we are now at the practical implementation stage of three main projects.

Access to the Multi-media Resources Centre

This project involves providing access to the possibility of consulting part of the Centre's library of 150,000 books and 5,700 periodicals on scientific and technical subjects, which cater for a readership of children and adults in search of information at all levels from the most elementary to the most highly specialized. Briefly, to describe the technical principle, this is based on computer configurations made up of scanners and software for the deciphering of letters, which analyse the visible print and transform it into data-processed signs. The microcomputer screen is then decoded by vocal synthesis or transitory braille terminals. Braille print-outs and a device giving access to a telematic data bank complete this equipment.

In the reading room, which is open to all categories of users, remote control enlargers are to be available to any readers suffering from defective vision, whether or not they belong to a given category of amblyopes. A team of librarians trained in the handling of the equipment and familiar with their problems will be there to assist visually handicapped readers.

The system for finding one's way

The CSI is located in an enormous building, with 30,000 square metres of exhibition space and a ceiling 42 metres high. The interior is so designed as to be totally open, both horizontally and vertically. Thus the noise reverberates from all directions and mingles in a swirl of sound, with no partitions or other flat surfaces to reflect it, and in this sort of spatial context a blind person is unable to exploit the system of orientation based on hearing and epidermic interaction. For this reason we are installing a system for guiding visitors, comprising two complementary features:

■ a system of paths which may be interpreted at ground level via the differences in materials and tactile patterns, and also the differences in colour for the benefit of the amblyopic;
■ sound signals indicating location broadcast individually by infra-red beams.

Access to permanent exhibits

The third project covers the specific problem of the contents of the permanent exhibition and the first phase of the programme is now being implemented. Basically the CSI presents its scientific information via interactive audio-visual methods.

About 70 per cent of films on the stands may be understood without seeing their pictures. However, directions for use should be added in braille on the controls, with diagrams in relief and more thorough explanatory texts on additional boards.

It is essential that the two forms of graphical expression, the one accessible to the eye and the other to the touch, should co-exist harmoniously from an aesthetic point of view, and for this reason the project is being made the object of an architectural survey and study in design. The material used for reproduction is to be plastic resin because of the reliability of the fine reliefs it provides, the satisfactory nature of its resistance and the broad range of colours and surface finishes.

We feel it is of paramount importance for braille to be – at last – a visible feature in a public cultural institution, so that its existence may become a familiar everyday feature. Too often it remains a symbol of blindness and thus creates a psychological stumbling block.

The preparation of the texts to go on the boards calls for re-writing of their essential contents in a condensed form, since space is limited. We are also transforming ordinary diagrams into tactile ones. But mere transposition cannot provide the specific elements for interpretation through touch. Sometimes there is a need to accentuate, simplify and explain the data, grade the degree of roughness of the surfaces in the light of the captions in colour and devise a way of expressing contrasts which will ensure easy and quick legibility. Fingers can detect particulars of shape and structure as fully as can the eye. All these are basic empirical tasks which are generally neglected in the specialized milieux in France.

Once a blind person can thus read unaided, he or she will no longer be dependent on the constricting and compulsory explanations, frequently of an analytical or impoverishing nature, of an escort who, however well-intentioned, will remain confined within the limits of what human effort can achieve.

The knowledge will thus be directly grasped via personal perception, without the possible incidental fatigue and overabundance or shortage of data. Moreover, the fact of personally perceiving the tactile version of the drawings will mean direct intelligibility without use of the vehicle of metaphors and analogies of an approximate nature. Generally the blind are obliged to put up with a wordy account in which the illustrations are described in a rambling manner and with reference to data which they do not possess.

Three-dimensional mock-ups, solid, and meaningful to the touch, are to complete the museographical equipment. The ideal size will not exceed 1.5 metres in full span, so that the two hands may constantly serve to provide a basis for an understanding of the proportions; the tactile approach necessitates an analysis via the breaking-down of the component parts and their mental recasting into a whole.

These special facilities are to be provided in the case of exhibitions which can be made basically accessible by aural or tactile means. One such exhibition is 'The World of Sound', which is a test case; we are going progressively to pursue the experiment in geology, exploration and conquest of the oceans and outer space, astronomy and mathematics, and also in the Inventorium where multisensorial devices are numerous. The exhibition on the subject of 'The Five Senses' is so designed as to incorporate the two forms of expression.

At the last stage, the information on accessibility should appear in the general press. Readers will in the normal course of things pass it on to the visually handicapped among their acquaintance, who will then themselves attend event belonging to the cultural heritage at the same time as everyone else.

In closing, I would like to draw attention to the fact that advances in publishing techniques and telecommunications are tending to increase the proliferation of visual information and to accentuate the physical and social taboo on touching. The visually handicapped may be given training which, though advanced, is based on words and devoid of concrete illustration. It would appear essential to set up a group for joint study and for joint action in different places so as to be able to offer the minority public concerned legitimate access to ethnographical, technological, artistic and architectural culture.

Paintings and visually impaired people

William Kirby

Since 1986 there has been a splendid growth in the involvement of visually impaired visitors to art galleries: there have been some fifteen sculpture-for-touch exhibitions in which they were able fully to share their perceptions with the artists and their sighted fellow-visitors. These exhibitions have shown an increased awareness of the special needs of visually impaired people, not only by making works available to touch but also by providing appropriate information and commentary, especially on tape, and by paying attention to contrasting backgrounds and lighting.

Two-dimensional work – painting, graphics and photography – is much less obviously accessible to those with poor sight. But two recent developments have shown how visually impaired people – those with low vision and even those with no sight at all – can share a perception and appreciation of the work of artists working on flat surfaces.

A partially sighted workshop to study paintings

The first workshop for partially sighted people to study paintings was held at the Whitechapel Gallery in London in February 1988. The exhibition was 'Fernand Léger – the Later Years'. I had visited the show on the opening day and confirmed my belief that Léger's work would, with its high contrast of line, shape and tone of colour and its big, bold shapes and figures, often outlined in contrasting colour, be partially visible to me with my peripheral sight – especially if I could have access to information and interpretation. I felt that the work could also be accessible to other kinds of low vision. So I suggested the workshop. The Whitechapel had recently held a very successful series of touch workshops for visually impaired people during the Jacob Epstein exhibition.

The Léger Workshop was attended by fourteen people, all registered blind or partially sighted. Their ages ranged from 14 to 35 and there were as many different eye conditions as there were participants – including a totally blind journalist. Their experience of art was also very mixed – three or four had had art school training whereas others had no acquaintance with art – especially with 'modern' art – or with visits to galleries.

The 20-minute gallery-guide to the exhibition had been recorded on tape cassettes. This taped introduction was posted to the participants so that they could study it beforehand. The full exhibition catalogue was put on tape by the Royal National Institute for the Blind Student Library for future reference and study.

The visitors were divided into groups of three or four and each group was accompanied by an artist who described, interpreted and discussed the work. The lighting level in the gallery was lifted for the two hours of viewing and the security and insurance barriers were removed under the supervision of the members of the gallery staff.

Round-table discussions preceded and followed the viewing and these showed how shared perceptions led to an insight into Léger's creative processes. The artists all commented on how much they had learned about the paintings by seeing them through partially sighted eyes. The participants were guided into the most difficult area – that of making subjective artistic and aesthetic judgements. Léger was not universally liked but the students' enthusiasm for the experiment and their demands for more workshops demonstrated how much they had learned.

That experiment and the subsequent Whitechapel workshops on Fontano Richard Deacon, and one to follow on Joan Miró, as well as a visually impaired workshop on Henry Moore at the Royal Academy, have not only shown that 'blind' people can gain from the experience of art, from paintings, in the case of Léger, and how much residual vision and the perceptions of totally blind people can be enriched: not only that, but these exhibitions and the workshops have identified fifty or sixty 'blind' people within striking distance of London who have now met others in similar situations to their own. They have all spoken of how they previously felt isolated in their frustrations about art, how they were not aware of things happening, and of how they all knew visually impaired people who thought there was nothing left in art galleries for them.

Fifty or sixty people in London is not a great number, but these are people whose expectations have been raised. Recent estimates from the Office of Population Censuses and Surveys have suggested that there are 1.75 million people in the UK with a severe or appreciable visual handicap. This amounts to 3 per cent of the population – far more than the 146,000 registered blind and 80,000 registered partially sighted in 1986. And forty-five people join the Register every week. These numbers make even more exciting the second development in 1988.

Living paintings: raised images and recorded commentaries

These paintings are being pioneered by the 'Living Paintings Trust'. The first set is related to ten paintings in the National Gallery. The paintings were selected because of how they can be used to teach visually impaired people about the two-dimensional illusions of space and perspective. Also, they have been chosen for either their strong story-line, linearity, contrasting elements of composition, visibility to the partially sighted or for their significance in the collection and in the history of art – or any combination of these elements.

It is expected that in the future galleries throughout the United Kingdom will have tactile paintings – and tactile images of sculpture, decorative arts, architecture, etc. from their own collections available for sale, loan and reference. They are highly recommended by all the people, both congenitally and adventitiously blind or partially sighted, who have either been advising the team producing the images or who have used them.

Each A4 thermoform image is accompanied by a printed reproduction and, absolutely essentially, by a taped recorded commentary which not only suggests how to 'read' the images, and describes the content of the painting, but also specifically addresses problems of perception and sight loss.

The raised images are not intended to be sculptures of the paintings but are meant to be an aid to achieving an insight into the artist's intentions or as a low-vision aid for partially sighted students of paintings.

Galleries and arts venues will wish to have the sets available, just as they sell National Gallery picture postcards and reproductions. It is foreseen that organizations will wish to make their own tactile paintings. The Trust will offer advice on the production of the models, thermoforms and the writing of commentaries; if the name of the Trust is to be associated with the production of tactile paintings they will be glad to offer advice and wish to exercise the kind of quality control that will help the makers of the models and the writers of the scripts to achieve the highest standards.

There is no sight without insight. There can be no substitute for actually seeing a painting, but for me 'Living Paintings' has meant that I can start to study paintings again; for others it will mean that they might be able to study paintings for the first time.

Touch exhibitions in the United Kingdom

Anne Pearson

Touch exhibitions really began in the United Kingdom in the 1970s. The early ones were confined to visually handicapped visitors, because of fears about conservation. More recently, however, they have almost always been integrated, i.e. open to everyone. This is partly because of the demand for them from the sighted public and partly because more has been learnt about the conservation precautions which can be used to protect objects from damage. Today the value of touch for every museum visitor is widely recognized and more and more experiments in tactile displays are taking place in museums large and small. Here, I shall refer only to a small minority of these.

The first major touch exhibition to be held in the United Kingdom was at the Tate Gallery in London in 1976. It was concerned with introducing modern western European sculpture to visually handicapped visitors and as such was seminal. It set the pattern for a kind of touch exhibition which is still continuing and developing. The sculptures, which included work by Henry Moore, Jacob Epstein, Barbara Hepworth and Edgar Degas, were arranged in a sequence from the more naturalistic to the more abstract. The first piece was a female nude and the last three were all abstract but with strong reference to the human figure.

This first Tate exhibition was followed by two more, both including works by leading contemporary sculptors. Other touch exhibitions of sculpture followed, in Cardiff, Nottingham and elsewhere. The exhibition called 'Said with Feeling' at the Castle Museum, Nottingham, was open to everyone and included pieces specially made for the exhibition by sculptors who firmly believed that their work should be handled to be truly understood and enjoyed.

'Beyond Appearances' was organized jointly by Nottingham Castle Museum and the Arts Council in 1985. It had sculptures by fifteen artists including Barry Flanagan, Anthony Gormley, Richard Deacon and

Kirsten Hearn. Kirsten Hearn is blind. Her sculpture was an installation in which the visitor was enclosed in swathes of felt while hearing the artist's experience of travelling on the London Underground. Other works were in a range of materials from marble, stone and wood to leather, newspaper and string.

More recently, in 1987, 'Revelations for the Hands' was held in Leeds City Art Gallery and in the University of Warwick Art Centre. It too was designed to give visually handicapped people access to great works of art. Pieces by Henry Moore, Randall-Page, Eduardo Paolozzi, Jacob Epstein, Barry Flanagan and John Skelton were all on display. In this exhibition, as in others, the same sculptures were preferred by blind and sighted visitors, although Epstein's *Deirdre*, with its exaggerated features, was particularly appreciated by visually handicapped visitors.

The most recent example of this kind of exhibition was held in Preston in the summer of 1988. It was about exploring sculptures which represent the human figure and featured work by Henry Moore, Elizabeth Frink and other famous sculptors as well as that of talented younger artists. It was in two parts. All the works in the main gallery could be explored by touch. Sculptures in a side gallery could not be touched because of their fragility, but they were carefully lit so that they could be enjoyed by visitors with residual vision.

One interesting thing about this exhibition was the preponderance of wood as medium. One of the largest works in this category was by Christine Kowal Post. It consisted of two 2.5-metre long carved reliefs expressing different emotions: love, joy, anxiety, grief, comfort and friendship. The sheer scale and detail of this limewood was much appreciated by blind visitors, although the composition was very complex and often difficult to interpret. At associated workshops for blind visitors held by the sculptress she handed round tools used for carving and this helped in the interpretation.

At the British Museum we have also held a touch exhibition with the human figure as its theme. Called 'The Human Touch', it was held in 1985 and used objects from a number of ancient cultures, to compare and contrast the various attitudes to and treatment of the human figure in widely differing artistic traditions. So, for example, we had a Jain saint – a nineteenth-century marble seated figure from Rajasthan – a highly stylized Nigerian male figure made of wood and a third-century BC female figurine from ancient Mesopotamia.

This wide-ranging choice cutting right across our vast collections was also the method we employed in our first exhibition held two years earlier and whose theme was animal sculpture.

In both these exhibitions our intention was different from that of the organizers of the modern sculpture exhibitions. Our primary concern was to introduce the visitors to the world from which the object came; to have them see and feel the sculpture not only as the creation of an individual artist but also as a product of its time and place. The object became therefore a catalyst between the visitor and the ancient world. Here we see touch taking on another significant function, that of demystifying agent, a way of breaking down barriers between our world and that of the remote past. Certainly many of our visitors were visibly moved by the experience of personally touching an object made by an unknown artist thousands of years ago.

Very different from any of these touch exhibitions was the one held at the Arnolfini Gallery in Bristol in 1987, entitled 'Feeling to See'. This was the first exhibition ever to be designed specifically for the blind and partially sighted; everything was made to be touched. In the first section contrasts of shapes, textures and surfaces translated into a tactile medium the juxtaposition of east and west conveyed in Shakespeare's *Antony and Cleopatra*. In the second section a giant apple was presented, first as a whole and then in all its component parts (skin, core, pips, etc.), through changes of scale and materials. In the third section the powers of a computer were demonstrated through a series of transformations in which an object began as a telephone handset and ended as a kettle. This unique exhibition was enjoyed equally by blind and sighted visitors.

Another important strand of touch exhibition development is the use of natural history collections. In 1981 the Ulster Museum in Belfast held one, using material from its zoology, botany and geology departments. It brought together minerals, crystals, sea-shells and sculptures in a way that invited the public to come and explore them and guess the identity of a mystery object. At the end of the month there were over three thousand entries from sighted people and ninety-six from the blind, clear evidence of the positive response from sighted visitors to the opportunity to touch.

The Natural History Museum in London has now held a few touch exhibitions. The first, in 1983, was called 'Exploring Woodland and Seashore'. It re-created the experience of walking through an English woodland and along the seashore. A taped commentary which included many animal sounds and bird songs described the wide range of models and specimens available to visitors for handling.

This survey of the many different types of touch exhibitions illustrates clearly the wide variety of ways in which our tactile sense is being used in museums and the consequent impossibility of saying anything useful which really applies to all of them. However there are practical considerations which must be allowed for if any touch exhibition is to work satisfactorily. They should be located on the ground floor of a museum, as near as possible to the entrance. There should be handrails or guide ropes linking the exhibits and braille and large print labels should be used. These labels should have a consistent layout in relation to the exhibits. Lighting should be strong and without glare. As far as possible thought should be given to providing a varying sensory experience, i.e. the objects should be alternately rough and smooth to relieve the fingers.

Most important of all, however, is the tape-guide. Many touch exhibitions have provided these to enable the visually handicapped visitor to enjoy the exhibition independently if he or she wishes, without the need for someone always on hand to explain and guide. Such tape-guides are not easy to write and much care and thought should be given to their content. It is not sufficient simply to record the panel copy and the labels. The tape should also provide clear orientation, should not be too long, and should use voices which are clear and attractive to listen to. More than one voice is a good idea, and the use of music and sound effects is also helpful.

We intend to build on all this experience, our own and others, as we prepare for our next touch exhibition, to be held in the spring of 1990. It is to be entitled 'The Way to the Forum' and, as this suggests, is about life in a Roman town. We will therefore have a good deal of Roman marble sculpture to be seen and felt, but also pottery, bronze, mosaics and wall-paintings. Touch will take its place as just one of the five senses and not be paramount as in our two earlier exhibitions. We will accentuate the accessibility of the exhibition to people with disabilities other than blindness, as well as to the able-bodied, by using music, taped information (for example, the sound of spoken Latin and Celtic), and by a series of dramatic presentations. The exhibition, therefore, will be an attempt to create a sense of what it was like to live in a Roman town of the second century AD, and will provide the focus for a wide range of educational activities, craft demonstrations, etc. For the first time at the British Museum we will also be experimenting seriously with reconstructions and replicas alongside actual artefacts. We intend to incorporate all the design features necessary to afford full participation for disabled people and will be involving artists with disabilities in the planning stage and during the exhibition itself.

In this short summary I have concentrated on describing touch exhibitions *per se*, which was my brief. There is much more going on, and workshops like those run by the sculptor Jefford Horrigan at the Whitechapel Art

Gallery in London, or the work of the Leicester University extra-mural department in teaching the skill of touch, could provide examples.

There is also a growing number of artists with visual handicaps who are organizing exhibitions of their own work, often using museums as venues. A recent example of this was the 'Eye for Art' exhibition held at the Gunnersbury Park Museum in West London. This was the first large-scale exhibition of paintings, photography and murals by visually handicapped artists to be held in the United Kingdom.

Blind children in the museums of Budapest, Hungary

Zoltan Gollesz

The teaching of history in primary schools should serve among other things to provide an ideological education. It affords a view of life in all its complexity and shows the relationship between politics and the historical context. Its mission is to provide a complete and objective portrait of each period in the evolution of mankind. In depicting a given epoch, history must not stop short at concrete events, or at comparative analyses of the different civilizations, ethnic groups and countries, with their respective cultures, languages, fine arts and popular art, architecture and urban or rural structures, morality, rules of etiquette, customs, dress, means of transport and long-distance communication – in short, at *whatever characterizes that epoch*. The portrayal of the age must also include the opinions of the people of that age concerning themselves and the world and the manner in which their view of life was reflected in the way they lived.

When history is taught to blind children it is obvious that for this purpose objects from everyday life, decorative objects and works of art must be used, together with anything else typical of the age, including weapons. And in the case of blind children it is most certainly desirable to introduce the musical world and the literature of the age.

From more than one point of view museums are the most suitable institutions for the portraying of periods of history.

1. For a blind child a lecture on the spot in a museum will provide a stronger impetus to learn than a lesson at school. The knowledge which can be acquired in school by verbal methods will be less readily committed to memory than that acquired through lectures in the museum; *here the atmosphere will be more informal and the communication will be more direct.*

2. There are almost unlimited possibilities for demonstrating the objec-

tive reality of a given age by placing *original objects* in the children's hands, and this itself will be an experience.

3. It is possible in this way to acquaint the pupils with the work of the *historian*, the *archaeologist* and the *restorer*.

4. From the educational point of view this method will have the positive effect of *rendering the museum attractive* and explaining its function and the services it can provide, thus imparting *the urge to educate oneself.*

5. Last but not least, the museum lectures provide an opportunity of *escaping from the closed universe* of a specialized educational institution with which the majority of blind children are obliged to content themselves.

In May 1986 the Primary School and Educational Institute for the Blind in Budapest concluded an agreement with the Department of Public Education of the National Museum. Under the terms of this the Museum provided regular fortnightly lectures for fourth-year pupils during the 1986–7 school year. The subject of the lectures was the prehistoric age. During the lectures and discussions the children were allowed to handle original finds – bones, stone implements and clay pottery. Later they were allowed to amuse themselves by making clay pottery, using a technique appropriate to their age, or were allowed to play at being archaeologists and discover finds by themselves in chests full of sand. They were also introduced to the work of the restorer and the mending of broken plates and were themselves allowed to try their hand at repair work.

In the light of the positive experience acquired at the National Museum we then contacted the Budapest History Museum, which is introducing fifth-year pupils in the same sort of way to the history of the Middle Ages with the help of its fine collections and with the aid of manual and make-believe activities. Together with the History Museum we arranged, for example, to enhance the lectures by an excursion to Aquincum. The Museum of War History is teaching modern history in a more serious form to sixth-form pupils.

In making use of this system at ascending levels, and in rendering the aforementioned institutions familiar and accessible to the pupils, our purpose is *to ensure continuity in such external assistance to the teaching of history.* Our further purpose in bringing history into the pupils' physical environment is to enable the knowledge they thus acquire to contribute to their integration into society and to provide the right sort of basis for their cultural integration.

We are seeking to maintain our co-operation with the aforementioned museums and to make a systematic practice of such joint work, while also investigating further possibilities.

We have entered into close association with the Professional Organization of Popular Museum Educators with a view to promoting links between the country's numerous museums and the institutions for the handicapped, and also by establishing more generally effective collaboration between the professions concerned, with a view to extending the benefit of such valuable aids to the teaching of history to the deaf and hard of hearing.

The purpose of this short introduction to our work is to establish international connections with a view to its future expansion. We are hoping that the specialists and the institutions involved will be prepared to send us documentary material, as we are willing to do on our side. Co-operation is perhaps the most effective means for promoting the cultural integration of the handicapped.

A current experiment at the Château de Blois, France: visits for the blind

Martine Tissier de Mallerais

Since the beginning of 1986 the Curatorial Department at the Château de Blois in the Val de Loire has been working with the Valentin Haüy Association on planning tours of the building specially adapted to suit the blind and the visually handicapped. By May 1987 we were able to receive our first blind visitors and last season their number had increased. We are not yet in possession of all the planned equipment, but we do have four vital accessories, namely, the relief ground-plan, the small-scale model of the château, casts of sculptures and the braille edition of the brochure.

On their arrival in the main courtyard of the château the groups of blind people are divided into sub-groups of three or four, each under the conduct of a voluntary guide still undergoing training and of a member of the curatorial staff; they are then asked to take their bearings and familiarize themselves with the layout of the buildings with the aid of a big relief ground-plan obtained by thermoform technique. To supplement this first general impression they next examine the model to be found inside the chapel of the château. This is on a scale of 1:100 (each of its sides measuring 1.40 metres), and is made of a strong plastic material perfectly suited to the repeated touching which is the basic means by which the non-sighted contrive to perceive spaces, volumes and forms. It is astounding to see how the blind explore, discover in detail and finally come to understand the albeit complex architecture of the château and the structural peculiarities of each wing. The model can be partially disassembled, so that they can also grasp the chronology of the building process, from the Middle Ages down to the seventeenth century. It is a remarkable teaching aid, not merely for the blind for whom it was originally intended, but for all the other visitors to the château.

It is planned to provide further detailed models to illustrate over-complex or excessively large architectural features (such as the Francis I staircase or the thirteenth-century great hall (the Salle des Etats)), so as to enable the non-sighted to grasp the significance of such features when they come to them. One of these is now being made; it will show the structure of the central pavilion of the Gaston d'Orléans wing with its oval dome and overhanging balcony crowning the monumental staircase. The other models await the necessary funds ...

For the actual tour of the buildings it has been necessary completely to alter the traditional explanations, to do away with any information of no interest to the blind and to find other subjects of comment more accessible to perception by the ear or the touch. Thus the spiral structure of the Francis I staircase may be conveyed by the sound of feet running down it, and the imposing proportions of the courtyard and great hall are suggested by their echoes – a principle to be used again for a musical background programme now being worked on. In the course of the visit appeal is primarily made to the specially strong tactile sensitivity of the blind. With the aid of one of them, Mr Alain David of the Blois branch of the Valentin Haüy Association, we have picked out, tried out and selected 'touchable' sculptures, mouldings and pieces of furniture which are readily accessible and sufficiently representative of the different styles, and these have been supplemented by a few small casts we found in our reserve collections. For the Gaston d'Orléans wing, whose finest sculptures, on the domed ceiling over the staircase, are out of reach, two big casts have been made, and these will also be of interest to the sighted visitor, since their distance precludes appreciation on the spot of the delicacy of the carvings.

Side by side with the institution of visits for blind people coming in groups, work is going ahead on a complementary project which will be operational in time for the 1989 tourist season. We were, in effect, concerned at being unable to provide a satisfactory welcome to blind people visiting the château individually and consequently without the assistance of a specialized guide. As a provisional measure until we can do better we have provided a four-page notice which is handed at the entrance to anyone accompanying a blind person. In the near future we are going to have a much more satisfactory arrangement. The firm of Directives Audiocom is at present working on an audio-guide system for the château which will exploit a pioneer technology and will primarily serve blind visitors coming independently: the latter will be provided with earphones and the sounds they hear will be emitted by the board, the picture or the piece of furniture in front of which they are standing. With this system it will be possible to tell the history of the château in a lively manner (with dramatized scenes, music and sound effects), suggest the atmospheres typical of the place and guide the fingers of blind visitors as they run them over a piece of furniture or a piece of sculpture, while at the same time warning them of such dangers in their path as steps, low doorways, etc.

A further feature of these arrangements for the blind is a braille brochure of which 2,000 copies have been made and which is on sale at a very reasonable price. It is the outcome of a joint effort pursued at great length by the Curatorial Department, Mr Alain David, the Paris headquarters of the Valentin Haüy Association and voluntary helpers. The brochure may be used during the actual visit, but in most cases it serves afterwards to remind visitors of what they have just been observing or help them to understand this more thoroughly. In addition to the text in braille the brochure contains a text in large type for persons with low vision and four illustrations in relief – a plan of the château and the royal emblems – produced by the thermoform process.

During the 1988 season the arrival of the first big groups of blind visitors, coming from all parts of France, but also from Italy, Germany, Denmark and elsewhere, raised a few problems not initially anticipated. The language barrier, which has so far been overcome case by case by calling in outside assistance from various quarters, is going to become much more of a problem if there is an increase in the number of groups from abroad and the number of languages involved. We see no other solution than to translate the recorded commentary now in preparation into several different languages at the enormous cost this will imply; one cannot hope to pay for this type of system out of the loan of headphones. A further point is that, in view of the size of most of the non-sighted groups, who come in coaches seating thirty-five to fifty people, we feel it is necessary to divide them up and to take some of the people first of all to a different part of the château for a different sort of visit, subsequently reversing the arrangement.

One of our museums is particularly suited to the non-sighted visitor: this is the archaeological museum on the ground floor of the Francis I wing, which mainly contains objects in relief. We have therefore prepared a scheme for fitting out this museum for the use of the blind and have entered it for the competition organized by the Direction des Musées de France for museums catering for blind visitors. In our own scheme each of the mural glass cases would be fitted below with a wide drawer in front of which blind visitors would be able to seat themselves on suitably designed stools. They would thus be given access to a fairly wide selection of original flints, pieces of pottery and miscellaneous tools, supplemented by a series of casts of those exhibits in the showcase which were too fragile to be handled or were unique of their kind. It is also planned to issue a braille catalogue.

The first season's visits for the blind led us to a further discovery. The groups which come from a distance, and especially those which come from abroad, all naturally come not merely to visit the Château de Blois but to spend one or more days in the Val de Loire area. We were at a loss as to what places to recommend as catering specially for the blind visitor and we feel that what is being attempted at Blois on the latter's behalf should not remain an isolated experiment; other historic buildings and other institutions in the area – possibly belonging to different cultural fields, natural history, for example, so as to preclude monotony – should in their turn provide facilities for the same specific public. We would thus be able to propose complete holidays in the Val de Loire area to our blind friends, with varied and complementary activities.

I would like to conclude by stressing how beneficial these visits for the blind can be, not merely – as is quite obvious – for the non-sighted, for whom they are primarily designed, but also for the guide-lecturers and even for the general public which chances to rub shoulders with the blind while the latter are exploring the building by tactile methods; in fact this is one of the reasons why I am not in favour of admitting the blind on special days or at special times. The education we receive does not give pride of place to touch, and we are capable of perceiving architecture and sculpture with our eyes alone, frequently in a highly intellectual way. The blind have a great deal to give us in this respect and they can teach us to rediscover the volumes, outlines and surface treatments in a more direct and sensitive way.

The Museum for the Blind in Brussels, Belgium

Micheline Ruyssinck and Mieke Van Raemdonck

The first initiatives designed to facilitate access to art for the visually handicapped took place in 1970 under the auspices of the Brussels Rotary Club. 'Art for the Non-Sighted' was an exhibition of authentic original sculptures rendered accessible through touch to the blind. The success of the event stimulated the organizers and prompted them to arrange a second exhibition in 1973, entitled 'Animals in Art'. Two years later, in October 1975, came the third one, 'Wood in the Hand of Man'.

Before analysing the successive stages in the history of the museum since its creation we must lay emphasis on the main original feature of this initiative, which consisted in offering the public authentic works of art from public or private collections. The task of organizing the exhibitions has been given to the Flemish-speaking and French-speaking education departments, which since 1978 have been alternately in charge, each in its turn thus having a whole two-year period over which to spread the heavy task of the preliminary research and the mounting of the exhibition itself.   At the outset exhibitions were of only brief duration and were held in rooms temporarily loaned by one or other of the curators, but since 1978 they have been lasting from eight to ten months and have been housed in a part of the museum now permanently assigned them.

The aforementioned exhibition on wood and its use was the first of a trio designed to permit readier recognition of the materials used for the different crafts and of the techniques adopted. A year later the second in the series gave a detailed introduction to work in stone, under the title of 'Stone: from Implement to Finished Work'. The third and final one which closed the series in 1977–8 was designed as an illustration to the subject of 'Earth and Metal'.

It was felt that visitors had now familiarized themselves with materials, and subsequent exhibitions were devoted rather to aspects of the history of art. Thus the one held in 1978–9 was entitled 'The Face Speaks'. This theme was at once a synopsis of the preceding exhibitions, since all the materials were involved, and a new departure, since it left technique aside and concentrated instead on the sociological aspect of form. The museum's collections were particularly suited to this new approach, since they were able to provide about sixty works representing all five continents and illustrating the diversity of the human face in all the wealth of its many historical and geographical metamorphoses.

The following year saw the exhibition on 'The Image of Buddha', which exploited the interest recently shown in non-European cultures. This time there was a given subject – Buddha – to be elucidated, within the context of a given culture, that of India. The exhibition was in two sections. The one was didactic in character and illustrated the life of Buddha with the aid of terracotta reliefs and wood, stone and bronze sculptures. In the other, original works and a map in relief illustrated the spread of Buddhism through eastern and south-eastern Asia. The quality of the works exhibited was of a standard high enough to bring out the oriental mysticism of the message conveyed by the attitude of the body, a phenomenon to which our public was particularly sensitive.

In 1980 the Europalia Committee, which every two years organizes a festival on the cultural legacy of one or other of the member countries of the European Community, devoted its biennial event to Belgium, to mark the 150th anniversary of the Belgian nation's birth. The occasion was celebrated by the Museum for the Blind by the holding of an exhibition entitled 'The *Belle Epoque* in Belgium', and this particularly prosperous period of our history was illustrated by furniture, clothing, sculpture, decorative objects and mock-ups.

In 1981 the Flemish-speaking education department took its cue from the findings of investigations which had revealed a public interest in architecture and it dealt with this subject in the exhibition entitled 'The Cathedral'. It was our blind visitors themselves who suggested that we organize an exhibition on architecture. Though architecture is a form of art with which they constantly come into contact, it is not easy for them to gain a clear idea of the structure of a building or of an architectural entity as a whole. Since the most detailed descriptions are unable to suffice, we needed to find practical means of providing as objective a picture as possible of what architecture signifies.

As our medium we chose the Gothic cathedral. This is a building of great interest from every point of view. To begin with, it has a structure which can be clearly understood. In addition, it occupies a predominant position in the town and embodies all the richness of our culture. And third, this latter fact enabled us to link up our exhibition with the ecclesiastical works of art to be found in our museum's very fine collections.

The idea was an attractive one, as much for the visually handicapped as for the museum itself. But it was also a bold one, and for this reason we did not hesitate to appeal to people who were both specialized in the matter and particularly concerned by the initiative. Thus it was that there was set up for the first time an advisory committee comprising among its members both non-sighted persons and educators from institutes for the blind. This body gave us some very valuable advice at different stages in the implementation of our project.

We were also able to rely on the assistance of the architect in charge of the restoration work at the cathedral in Mechelen (Malines), which is one of our finest. The restoration work there had made available a mine of data and documentary material on the building, to which we were given access: ground plans and detailed cross-sections, architectural fragments and such pieces of equipment as wheelbarrows used by stone-masons or stone-cutters. It was for this reason that St Rombaut was chosen as the typical cathedral for purposes of illustrating our subject.

The exhibition in its final version was composed of two sections. One of these showed the preparations for building a medieval cathedral in stone, and the building process itself. There were plans and sketches made by the master craftsmen of the Middle Ages, a number of different hammers and chisels used by stone-cutters, original architectural fragments such as a balustrade and a pinnacle, a fourteenth-century statue of an angel from Mechelen and a gargoyle. The contractor in charge of the restoration work at Mechelen also provided us with three reconstructions of a finial, each illustrating a different stage in the work.

The other section was devoted to architecture as such and contained mock-ups, small-scale models and reliefs carved in wood. We had chosen wood for practical reasons: it is easy to cut and polish, and furthermore it is pleasant to touch. The central exhibit was a big mock-up of the cathedral 227cm long and 190cm high (if we include the tower), on a scale of 1:50. This showed the outside of the building. The interior of the cathedral was illustrated by a model of one bay, made to this scale, and a relief ground-plan gave a general idea of the whole. Three versions of the Gothic window served to indicate how style developed. To all this we added two reconstructions of arches, one Romanesque and the other Gothic, and a small model of the cathedral on a more reduced scale (1:500) to give an immediate idea of the whole.

The individual visitor was provided with a cassette and reader with which to hear a description of the objects exhibited recorded against a background of music and of sounds of building work. However, most visitors preferred a guided visit. In that case they could also touch a dozen carefully chosen objects from the Medieval Art Industries and Sculpture section of the museum.

A further activity certainly deserves mention, and this is the guided tour of the cathedral of St Rombaut, which enabled the visually handicapped who had visited the exhibition in the museum to compare their impressions with the reality. They spread their arms to measure the size of the real spaces and could then refer back to the model of the bay, which had been specially brought to Mechelen. The climb to the top of the 97-metre tower and the exploration of the many bells and of the mechanism working the carillon were extraordinary experiences for everyone.

We may proudly say that the reactions were positive. Several blind or partially sighted people came back more than once to visit the exhibition. A cause for great surprise was that sighted people came likewise to congratulate and thank us, explaining that they had been attracted by the clear and well-thought-out character of the exhibition, which had enabled them to see a great and impressive building in a new way. They had also marvelled at seeing an exhibition containing no glass cases or 'do not touch' labels. Teachers found the exhibition an excellent aid to their explanations of Gothic art. We had thus reached a wider public than initially intended.

On 7 April 1982 our Department won the 'European Museum of the Year' Award, an annual prize awarded by the Bank of Ireland. Since then the exhibition has travelled, first of all inside Belgium and subsequently in the Netherlands, finally going to Vienna and Berlin. We intend shortly to house it permanently in one of the rooms of our museum.

The year 1982–3 was the year of 'Europalia Greece', and the French-speaking education department, anxious to take part in the event, presented 'Woman: a Trilogy'. This exhibition, a large portion of which was devoted to classical antiquity, was designed to illustrate and analyse the successive changes in the representation of the female body, demonstrating from both the aesthetic and the historical point of view the relation between these changes and the changes in woman's status in society. Visitors to the exhibition were also taken round the permanent collections.

An assessment of the achievements of all these exhibitions was made at the European symposium on tactile layouts of towns, in 1984, and a year later an animal sculpture exhibition entitled 'The Sacred Animal and the

Museums and people with impaired vision

Animal as a Symbol' opened its doors. In view of the almost infinite possibilities afforded by the general subject of animal sculpture the organizers had confined themselves to the one specific aspect consisting in the almost ritual relations entertained between man and animal, as illustrated in the Egyptian, Chinese, Mexican and Christian cultures.

The organizers of all these exhibitions have been seeking to give the visually handicapped an ever-increasing share in the activities of our museums, and other experiments, too, have been attempted. Thus arrangements are made for the ordinary temporary exhibitions to be visited by the blind where their contents so permit; or else, partitioned educational units are installed inside permanent exhibition rooms.

One of these units has been put up in the section devoted to the Near East. It contains not only maps made in relief and small-scale models, but also some authentic original objects (pottery, small sculptures and cylinder seals) which are placed in specially designed glass cases easily openable during guided visits. The same system has been adopted for a second unit in the India rooms.

These initiatives are a response to the wish expressed by the blind themselves, who want as far as possible to be a part of the normal life of the museum. The attempt to fulfil this wish certainly raises a number of museographical problems, since exhibits must not be allowed to suffer harm from being touched and since the galleries must remain attractive to the sighted visitor.

In 1987 the 'James Cook and the Pacific' exhibition was held. The organizers, anxious to present this subject in full both to the visually handicapped and to the sighted public, had paid particular attention to the aesthetic aspect of the whole. The exhibition was in four sections, dealing respectively with the life of James Cook, his Pacific expeditions, the clash between the different cultures and the cultural features by which the navigator was particularly impressed.

The exhibition held in March 1988, which was entitled 'Coachman, crack your whip!', gave us the opportunity to present the public with some carefully chosen pieces from among our museum's big collection of fully harnessed coaches and carriages. The subject is perhaps a more easily accessible one, and the exhibition did not merely give pride of place to a few fine eighteenth- and nineteenth-century vehicles but also attempted to explain the basic components of the horse-drawn carriage and how they evolved in the course of time, with the aid of small-scale models, explanatory texts and original objects.

138

The Royal Art and History Museums are among the first institutions to have organized events for the non-sighted. They are to be congratulated on adopting for the purpose the hitherto unprecedented practice of including in the exhibits original works taken directly from their own collections. The wager laid in 1975 that it would be possible to mount a yearly exhibition accessible to the blind on premises set aside and specially fitted out for the purpose was thus to point the way to a whole series of subsequent initiatives.

The problems which have arisen and which continue to arise are of many different kinds. The first – and perhaps the hardest to resolve – lies in the antagonism between the claims of conservation and the need for the public to be able to touch the exhibits. The consequence is that the criteria for selection are of necessity extremely strict and are primarily connected with the nature of the material. A further criterion is the 'readability' of the work. This is above all a matter of size. The visitors must be able, while remaining in a comfortable position, to explore the exhibit in its entirety and in detail, and this automatically rules out works that are too large or too small; in this latter case they will be unable to perceive the fine details of the relief carving. A third point is that it is preferable for an exhibit to be in a good state of conservation, since any mutilation will create a feeling of unease and be an obstacle to overall understanding of the work.

A further difficulty that has been encountered is that of the level of the dialogue which can be established between the guide-lecturer – holder of a degree in art history and archaeology – and the group of visitors. By reason of the slowness of exploration by touch, the fact that most of the visitors have no 'art history memory', and hence no basis of reference, and also the varied nature of the public, we have had to devise a special guided visit technique, which has progressively taken shape and developed with the many kinds of experience acquired in practice.

The guided visits, in which a guide-lecturer takes charge of a group of five people – and which are so designed as to enable each member of the group to derive the maximum benefit from the experience – are free of charge and are arranged by the education departments on request. Literature, on sale at a minimum charge, consists of catalogues (in braille or printed in black and white) and illustrations produced by the thermoform technique, and also tape recordings are available in some cases.

Receiving visually handicapped and non-sighted children at the Natural History Museum in Bordeaux, France

Janine Prudhomme

One of the aims our institution has set itself is to have children discover the animal world and, once they have discovered it, teach them to understand nature and instil into them respect for their environment.

Our daily practice in pursuit of this objective with children of the last two years in primary school set us thinking about disabled children, particularly the visually handicapped and non-sighted, and a special programme of activities has now been arranged for these. This programme has so far been carried out with groups of twenty to thirty children, i.e. two classes at once; the arrangement derives from the fact that the institution from which they come is in an outlying suburb of Bordeaux and is obliged to hire a coach to bring them in.

Since we need to remove the stuffed animals from their showcases we are compelled to arrange for the children to come on Tuesdays when the museum is closed to the public and to appeal for assistance in shepherding them round to those of our attendants who are prepared to sacrifice their weekly day off – which they do willingly in such circumstances.

In children with very low vision or no vision at all the other senses are particularly well developed, and those we need to exploit to a maximum are touch and hearing.

After meeting the teachers and deciding with them on a selection of specimens chosen in the light of the animal species referred to in the natural sciences or French syllabus, and also of the animal sounds the children hear as a part of their everyday background, we make the appointment and in due course remove the specimens from their showcases. Handling is important because many of the animals are large and all are fragile.

Sometimes the visit is preceded or followed by a walk round the zoo, where the smell peculiar to each animal will add to what can be learned through touch and hearing.

Recognizing animals by touch

The initial contact with the animals in the museum is always a source of wonderment. The children's light fingers explore the furs, distinguish between the llama's thick woolly fleece, the soft smooth coat of the seal and the rough hairy coat of the wolf, compare the hedgehog's prickles with those of the porcupine, and play with the gorilla's hands, but hesitate to feel the poison fangs of the snakes! Particular importance is assigned to the birds. On their first visit the children will content themselves with 'seeing' (to use their own term) the birds of prey with their talons and sharp beaks.

But the visit would be incomplete if the King of Beasts himself did not receive our young guests. Here the difficulty starts, because this star exhibit is too large and heavy to be moved; never mind, he will stay in his showcase and the children will go inside to greet him, stroke his mane, touch his claws and fangs and find that, even by opening their arms as wide as they possibly can, they will be unable to reach from his hindquarters to his muzzle.

Two hours scarcely suffice for all these discoveries, and the visit will come to an end after the hands dirtied by all the stroking of furs and feelings of feathers have all been carefully washed.

Recognizing birds by ear

A second visit will serve to familiarize the children with their environment. Their institution lies in grounds with a bird population representative of a large number of species common to all our gardens. Our work will consist in giving an identity to each singer and suggesting an appearance, volume and size, before finally giving a name and determining the bird's eating habits: its beak will show whether it is insectivorous or granivorous. For this purpose we have recorded bird songs and then edited our recordings so as to obtain sufficiently long sequences for the children to have time to assimilate the sound while holding the bird. For the system to be effective the children must listen in small groups of five or six, each child being provided with a specimen. Four or five different species will suffice per group and two or three groups are accommodated on each floor of the museum.

The children are most attentive and the results obtained are encouraging. When they are later made to listen to a bird song chosen at random on the tape they are supposed not merely to find the name of the bird but also find the bird itself among the specimens laid out on the table. Errors are very rare, and very often the children are quite capable of imitating the song they have heard.

It must naturally always be borne in mind that stuffed animals are fragile and are liable to suffer from too frequent handling; the specimens need careful selecting. But if at the end of the visit the owl is a bit more ruffled than usual and looks rather comical the skilled hands of the taxidermist will put things to rights: what are a few hours of extra work compared with the children's enjoyment?

The tactile museum at the Lighthouse for the Blind in Athens, Greece

Iphigenia Benaki

Some definition or clarification of the term 'tactile museum' would appear to be necessary from the start, to preclude possible misunderstandings or misinterpretations of the nature of our institution.

The word 'museum' is a word of Greek origin which means 'realm of the muses', and we can well understand its use in connection with a tactile museum of art. Thus we may say that the contents of our museum form a normal and as far as possible a representative collection of works of art made neither by, nor specially for, the blind, but that all may be touched and all provide equal access and equal opportunities for enjoyment to blind and sighted alike. The only special feature of the institution lies in the arrangement and placing of the various exhibits, which are intended to afford safe maximum access with minimum risk for blind people who wish to touch, explore or handle the objects in a manner suited to their individual level of perception and aesthetic appreciation.

The main impetus and the chief motivation behind the establishment of a museum facility for the blind lay in the desire to secure access for the blind to the world of art so as to help them acquire an objective knowledge of art appreciation and develop an aesthetic life previously badly hampered by the regulations in force in ordinary museums and by the general social environment. It should be pointed out here that the most difficult problem in the education of the blind has always been precisely that of the development of their aesthetic life as an essential aspect of their personality as a whole.

Attempts by educators to use classroom descriptions as a means of discharging their responsibility in this important area have proved not only unsuccessful but actually confusing. Verbal description, no matter how detailed or how carefully rehearsed, cannot be a substitute for concrete objective experience; the most it can achieve is a meaningless repetitive verbalism empty of any real comprehension of the true values, whether the subject is works of art or architecture or natural history or other physical phenomena.

Having become aware of the failure of this verbal descriptive method, as early as the last quarter of the nineteenth century educators of the blind conceived the idea of using special models for the exploitation of tactile educational methods. But despite their undeniable value the school collections used did not, for various reasons, provide a satisfactory answer to the problem. And yet the French philosopher Diderot, in evaluating the senses, writes: 'I found that of the senses the eye is the most superficial, the ear the most arrogant, smell the most voluptuous, taste the most superstitious and fickle, touch the most profound and philosophical.' And Michael Anagnos, a distinguished Greek educator who emigrated to the USA and became the second director of the famous Perkins Institution for the Blind in Boston, writes in his report dated 1897:

> Tactual observation is of inestimable value. It bridges over the chasm from the known to the unknown, from the concrete to the abstract, and lays a solid foundation for the mind to work upon. It arouses the attention of the blind and excites their interest. It appeals to experience and stimulates their powers of observation to intense activity. It feeds the mind with real food and raises it out of the slough of inattention and listless inactivity.

In recent years serious efforts have been made to build up larger and more meaningful collections, but they have been severely criticized as contributing to the isolation of the blind and running counter to the modern philosophy of total social integration for the disabled. Such a system requires that all persons, regardless of their physical condition, should enjoy exactly the same rights and opportunities as the rest of the population under normal integrated programmes covering all aspects and activities of the life of the nation.

The Lighthouse for the Blind, although both on principle and in practice always a staunch champion of the integration ideal, nevertheless recognizes that its universal application is not yet possible. Efforts in various parts of the world to achieve full integration for the blind as visitors to exhibitions and to permanent collections have met with insurmountable difficulties, because most of the time it has not been possible to touch the objects, as is quite understandable. All the above views, ideas and problems were repeatedly discussed in detail among the members of the Board of Directors of the Lighthouse and other interested friends, and all the pros and cons of proposed possible solutions were considered and analysed. These discussions led us to two conclusions. The first was that there existed a crying need to objectify the experience and knowledge of blind people by bringing within reach of their hands as many of the objects and creations of the surrounding world as possible. The second was that this could best be done through the establishment of a tactile museum facility, which, in addition to catering for the basic need for real experience and knowledge of the objective world, would provide access to an effective contact with important creative works of art; these in their turn would provide the appropriate stimulus for an appreciation of art and the development of an aesthetic life related to the visitor's social environment.

With this in view, and after making the necessary preparations, establishing the necessary contacts and securing the valuable assistance and guidance of Professor Alkmini Natsouli-Stavride of Athens, the distinguished woman archaeologist, we proceeded to organize our tactile museum in the neo-classical Lighthouse. We need make no mention here of the financial, organizational and technical difficulties we faced when seeking to acquire the exhibits needed for the building-up of a meaningful initial collection for our newly born project. I can only say here that, availing ourselves of the assistance of friendly organizations, we concentrated at the initial stage on acquiring a representative collection of classical works of art. Thus exact copies of the most important statues, bas-reliefs, vases and so on, were reproduced and displayed in a manner enabling blind people from all parts of the world to enjoy the aesthetic appeal of ancient Greek treasures of successive ages.

The collection covers the periods from the age of Cycladic art to the Hellenistic age and provides an overview of the most important of the ancient Greek masterpieces whose originals are to be found in different museums in Greece and abroad. For this reason it does more than contribute to the development of the knowledge and personality of the blind: it also attracts schools for sighted children, who visit us in order to obtain a general view of the exhibits as an educational and cultural experience. Their visits provide an excellent opportunity for sighted children and adults to associate with the blind, which is the most effective means of promoting the ideal of social integration.

From the very beginning the tactile museum elicited a wide response from abroad, and this continues to grow as it becomes better known. Large numbers of both blind and sighted individuals, and groups from universities or associations in a variety of countries, have visited us out of a desire to assess the artistic value of these famous classical treasures at close quarters and sense the rapture they radiate.

A special feature which also attracts the interest of visitors is a collection of paintings by blind and partially sighted children from fourteen coun-

Museums and people with impaired vision

tries. These paintings are the result of a research project undertaken by the International Exhibition Centre for Children's Paintings.

Our museum aspires to create, over and above its significant collection of works of art, sections devoted to folk cultures, natural history, architecture and technology, as well as a section for appliances and aids used in the past for the education of the blind. Its programme includes periodical exhibitions illustrating the evolution of human civilization. Naturally all such plans develop at a rate proportionate to our ability to secure the necessary funds. Our immediate priority at the present time is the creation of a model exactly reproducing the rock of the Acropolis as it now is, with all its monuments. Precautions have been taken to ensure that the model of the Parthenon we have already acquired fits into its place on the model of the rock. We feel that such a remarkable acquisition will be of inestimable value and will arouse worldwide interest: we also feel that the importance of this project justifies our pressing appeal for funds to the Ministry of Culture and other appropriate authorities and institutions, as well as to individuals who may be interested in seeing such an inspiring idea and initiative materialize.

In our catalogue, printed in large type and in Greek, English and German, details are given of all the exhibits in the tactile museum. Catalogues also exist, of course, in braille, in both Greek and English. We have further found it helpful to label every exhibit properly in braille and in ordinary print.

The museum is open to visitors on Wednesdays, but visits can also be arranged by appointment on other days of the week. Under the special regulations for blind visitors each group placed in the charge of a special guide should consist of no more four people with their escort.

In concluding this paper I would like to convey to you some idea of the delight experienced by blind visitors, whether children or adults, as they cleverly run their hands over a statue and with sensitive fingers seek to examine its every curve and counter-curve and its every fine detail. At the moment when the stimulus of the artist's design establishes a direct relationship with the subjective ability of the observers to appreciate grace and beauty in art, you can see their expression change and their faces light up, as they probe ever deeper as though trying to absorb all the values of the culture that produced such masterpieces.

The tactile museum in Budapest, Hungary

Emese Szoleczky

It is the western museums whose educational methods for the public have been responsible for spreading abroad the astonishing idea of specially organizing a museum activity for the blind whenever and wherever the contents of an exhibition may be touched.

We at our museum are proud of the fact that in 1984 it became one of the first in Hungary to provide the opportunity for blind people to become acquainted with its exhibits. We have great pleasure in observing that not only are the winter meetings for adults organized by the Wesselényi Sports Centre of the National Organization for the Blind and Visually Handicapped (VGYOSZ) well attended by the young, but that these museum events have also been brought to the knowledge of the blind school, whose pupils can attend them in conjunction with their lessons at school.

Our aim here is to give an overall picture of work in the Hungarian museum, including both its successes and its difficulties. In our museum the majority of the exhibits are displayed under glass, so that we can hardly use them for educational purposes. Instead of a mere walk through the exhibitions rooms, we therefore organize lectures on the special sections of our museum and on certain objects, and these are given by our professional staff. For example, during the lecture on our collection of flags and regimental colours both the historical evolution of these and the connection between heraldry and vexillology were discussed. On such occasions the visitors are allowed to touch both original objects and copies. Hence in this instance the group became acquainted in detail with the history of the museum, its library and the numismatic and flag collections.

Our meetings with adults are unusual in many ways. As a general principle, eight to ten persons are considered to be the optimal number in a group; but the audience for a lecture combined with the presenting of objects usually numbers between twenty and forty. Since these lectures are held on Saturdays they have become family events. We would say that one of the reasons for their popularity lies in our readiness to fall in with the visitors' ideas and wishes, and in planning the topics for each subsequent year's lectures we take their requests into consideration. Sometimes the lecture ends with an informal conversation, or the lecturer is assailed with questions, and if because of these we cannot finish what we have planned to say nobody will despair; we will continue next time. We hope these events will be as successful in the future as they have been in the past.

In our educational work for the public one of our chief aims is to make the children like and understand the museum. We have therefore made an effort to take part in the general education and the teaching of history in schools for visually handicapped children. Under a recent agreement with the Elementary and Boarding School for the Blind two parallel classes are to visit us eight times each to learn about the main events in the modern history of Hungary. To our delight it was the teachers of the school who asked for such co-operation and they also decided on the topics of the lectures. Since it is very important for pupils to have a permanent connection with museums we are also – together with the National Museum and the Budapest History Museum – providing a series of lectures for fifth- and sixth-year pupils.

Learning with all the senses

Angelika Schmidt-Herwig

'Learning with all the senses' is the title given by the education department of the Museum of Prehistory and Protohistory in Frankfurt-on-Main to its system of museum education.

In the new rooms made available for the purpose in 1987 at No. 3 Weissfrauenstrasse – we have christened them 'the Molehill' – preparatory talks are held in the mornings for pupils who wish to visit the museum as part of their school course. All are equally welcome, whether they come as pupils of vocational schools, as members of classes in practical work or as history, art or Latin students. In the afternoons the rooms are open to visitors of all ages – children, adolescents and adults.

At most of the preparatory talks the 'Molehill' provides originals to be looked at, understood and investigated. We arrange programmes in which the archaeological find and its original context are made the central object of our investigations, and here the pupils need to make use not only of their eyes and voices but also of their sense of touch, smell and taste for a practical understanding of what they are taught.

The conclusions we have drawn from our realization of the importance of all the senses and from their use in this way have led us to turn our attention to those groups of visitors for which, in purportedly 'normal' circumstances, the study of archaeological finds is out of the question or remains restricted, namely, the disabled. We now provide guided visits for the blind and visually handicapped in our permanent exhibition rooms; for example, there is a tour of the department of Roman sculpture entitled 'The world of the gods and the cult of Mithras in Roman Nida'. An exhibition room in the 'Molehill' is further set aside for small temporary shows accessible alike to sighted, visually handicapped and blind visitors; one such exhibition is now on schedule on the subject of prehistoric man's impact on nature and the environment.

Museums and people with impaired vision

In our view it is perfectly possible in an archaeological museum to provide educational aids which are suited alike to blind, visually handicapped and sighted people. Thus in co-operation with the German School for the Blind in Marburg/Lahn a portable 'suitcase exhibit' has been produced whose subject is the dwelling house in the neolithic age. This is a model of a Hessian house of the Ribboned Ware period and is made to a scale of 1:50; it consists of ready-made components to be assembled on a ground plan made in relief. The separate members – gable, posts, side walls and roofing – have to a large extent been made of natural materials.

Before being set up in the Museum of Prehistory and Protohistory this model most successfully passed tests for stability and for the logicality of its assembly system when tried out by two different classes in the Carl Strehl School for the Blind and Visually Handicapped in Marburg/Lahn. It is arousing great interest among sighted pupils as well, and, by explaining the significance of the raised dots used in braille, we are able to give these pupils an understanding of the way blind and visually handicapped pupils do their work.

V

Museums and people with impaired hearing

The deaf

Bernard Mottez

The situation of a deaf person will vary according to his or her degree of deafness. Obviously someone who is merely a little hard of hearing or even partially deaf will not be handicapped in the same way as a very deaf person – let alone a person who is stone deaf – especially if he or she can be fitted with a hearing aid. Stone deaf people are quite incapable of hearing the spoken word and must rely on lip-reading.

Lip-reading is a difficult task, and not all deaf people are good at it by any means. Not every word is legible via the movement of the lips, and there are words which look so alike as to be indistinguishable except in the appropriate context. The lip movements of each new speaker have to be studied specially, and speakers do not all use their lips in a way that provides for equal ease of lip-reading. Some people articulate poorly, scarcely opening their mouths, have lips which are too narrow, or half hide their lips behind a beard or a moustache. Guessing what words are being spoken and trying to follow necessitate such an effort that the deaf person is scarcely at liberty to join naturally in a conversation. Lip-reading is tiring and cannot be kept up for too long; where more than three people are talking together it is a distinctly doubtful possibility. It is naturally out of the question in the case of a public lecture, a radio broadcast or even a television programme.

There is also the other side of the dialogue to be considered. The difficulty for deaf people to say what they have to say, take part in an oral conversation, get themselves accepted and have themselves listened to does not derive purely from the trouble they have in following what is said. Since they will lack some of the points of reference they will constantly commit breaches of the rules of conversation and their remarks will not always be to the point. There is more to it still. Many deaf people, owing either to the nature of their voice, their elocution or even the inadequacy of their knowledge of the spoken language, cannot be understood by those around them. In the lives of deaf people the problem of making themselves heard weighs at least as heavily as the feeling of frustration at being unable to hear other people. This explains why many deaf people are lonely, especially if they have become deaf late in life.

For in fact the situation of the deaf person will also be dependent – and primarily so – on the age at which the deafness has occurred. Sometimes the dividing line is drawn between those who were born deaf or became so before learning to speak and those whose deafness dates from later in life. The former will necessarily have learned to speak by artificial means; but those who have become deaf in the course of their childhood or in very early adolescence tend to share the same fate. They will have been educated at the same schools and will likewise spend all their lives in the deaf community, where they will make their best friends and choose their life partner (since only about 10 per cent marry non-deaf people). They will derive immense enjoyment from the social events so eagerly sought by deaf people; these may take place in the centres which exist in most of the world's major towns, or may take the form of sporting events – whether local matches or the Olympic Games attended by thousands of deaf from all parts of the world – or of dinner-parties or performances at special theatres.

For those who have become deaf after completing their schooling – and who are generally referred to as having 'lost their hearing' – things are quite different. It is rare for them to mix with the aforementioned people, formerly referred to as 'deaf and dumb' even when they are able to speak.

It is true that the term 'deaf and dumb' is tending to fall into disuse. Yet those concerned still use it in their own language to describe themselves, since they touch first their ear and then their mouth with their index finger. They indeed possess a language of their own by which they are able to communicate without difficulty and on equal footing by means of gestures. This is the sign language, formerly known as the 'deaf-and-dumb language'. It is a language which varies slightly from one region to another and varies above all from country to country. Thus since about 1973 it has been customary to state whether what is being used is the ASL (American Sign Language), or the LSF (French Sign Language), etc. However the deaf of all countries in the world have an astounding ability to improvise a common language on the spot when they meet each other. This explains the fairly international character of the deaf community. Its members are great travellers.

Deaf children whose parents are deaf will naturally learn their language from their parents at home. Such cases represent a minority, estimated at about 10 per cent. Most deaf children will have learnt the language at a special boarding school, not from their teachers, who have made it a point of honour to ignore the language's existence ever since a congress famous for its disastrous decision (Milan, 1880) banished it from the classroom, but from their seniors in the playground and dormitories. Here it will have been the language of conspiracy and of expressions of emotion – the language of children leagued against non-deaf teachers.

But since the early 1970s the sign language has been tending to recover its right to existence, and so have the deaf. They are beginning once more to occupy posts formerly denied them, in the education of the deaf in particular. They now teach their language to those who can hear, on a growing scale. And now that interpreters are more frequent they are beginning to be able to play a larger part in the social, political and cultural life of the nation.

Sufferers from defective hearing and the new techniques for communication

Eric Bizaguet

I am going to talk about people who suffer from defective hearing but are able to analyse the spoken word well enough to understand it without lip-reading or gestures. My subject will be those who are hard of hearing and not the deaf, for the two cases are different.

People with defective hearing fall into several different groups. In France their overall number is 3,800,000. Most of them – two million – are only slightly affected, and of these the majority are people over seventy. They manage to understand when they talk to someone they can look straight in the face, but in adverse surroundings the slightly or moderately deaf person will be unable to follow a conversation, particularly if unacquainted with the subject being discussed and so unable to fill the gaps from mental sources. When I visit a museum I have no such mental means of filling the gaps, and in some museums I am 'culturally disabled'.

The 3,800,000 or so people with slightly, moderately or badly affected hearing may be rehabilitated with the assistance of a hearing aid. Some are willing to use one, while others are not. There are 110,000 totally deaf people who can be fitted with a device but are unable to understand without lip-reading and thus very frequently need to use the sign language.

In general, people who have partially lost their hearing are unconscious of the fact. What are the first warning symptoms? They will complain that people are not articulating clearly enough, or are talking too fast. Their deficiencies need to be analysed and compensated for. During museum visits the guides make no allowance whatsoever for this phenomenon, and it is very difficult to ask them to speak more loudly, so that a substitute will need to be found. The most important symptom is a general refusal to visit anything or go anywhere: people who are growing deaf will remain shut up in their homes because they are afraid of showing themselves to be failures. It is fairly easy to help them if their deafness is slight, moderate or even severe via the use of technical devices which are relatively inexpensive considering the results they can provide. A final point is that all deaf people have worse difficulties in a noisy atmosphere: they will understand on an average only 20 per cent of the words spoken to them, whereas to understand a conversation one will need to hear at least 80 per cent. A hearing aid will enable them to isolate the voice of the person they are talking to and to arrive at a better signal/sound ratio and thus at a more complete understanding.

The figure of 3,800,000 for the deaf population of France would appear to be enormous. It should be realized that one's hearing begins to decline at the age of twenty and that the deficiency increases with age. All of us have people in our families who are to be seen making a slight effort to hear. There is nothing to be ashamed of about this: the only problem is that we always tend to imagine that poor hearing is concomitant with a decline in intellectual faculties. This idea is ingrained in the minds of elderly people, who refuse to acknowledge that they are losing their hearing for fear of being considered intellectually lacking at the same time. This is a serious error, and there should be a campaign to demonstrate that a hearing aid may be necessary at any age.

Inability or ability to hear what one is told is thus dependent on three factors. There is first of all the individual hearing defect: the person may be slightly, moderately or severely deaf and the sounds reaching him or her may or may not be distorted. Then there is the environment: in a lecture hall, for example, a deaf person may have great difficulty in understanding the speaker, since such rooms have a great deal of resonance. An elderly person whom you take to church may tell you that he or she can no longer understand mass; the reason will be that the quality of the sound is poor. A further point is the deaf person's position within his or her surroundings and the noise or absence of noise going on all around. Obviously, during a guided visit, for example, a deaf person must stand near the guide and not at the opposite end of the room. The third factor lies in the nature and quality of the hearing aid, if any, and I am now going to describe some of the possible devices.

Three systems which may help to overcome a hearing difficulty when visiting a museum or a theatre

1 **Magnetic induction** To produce magnetic induction one must wire the whole room. The words spoken are picked up by a microphone and fed into an amplifier connected with a magnetic loop. This creates a magnetic field within the room which is conveyed to the hearing aid, whose owner can thus hear what has been said, whatever his or her position within the magnetic loop. The normal acoustics of the room will

no longer be operative. The advantage is that this equipment is very inexpensive: it will suffice to purchase an amplifier and some electric wire. The problems are that, first, the deaf person must wear a hearing aid capable of being turned to a 'telephone' position (which is not always the case) and, second, two magnetic loops cannot be installed side by side: the system cannot therefore function properly if there are six rooms to be visited. On the other hand, if one considers the quality/price ratio it is the best choice for a lecture hall. It is tending, however, to be less used because the deaf are increasingly adopting aids worn inside the ear which do not possess the necessary telephone coil.

2 High-frequency communication This is a sort of walkie-talkie system adapted for the use of the deaf. A live voice or a recording is transmitted via an HF transmitter. The deaf, standing opposite, hear the words on wires reaching right up to their ears (they must have a hearing aid with telephone coil). They will hear the voice directly, since the HF transmitter will convey it to their ears by magnetic induction. They will also hear it as clearly as though the speaker were standing thirty centimetres away, though he or she may actually be at a distance of up to fifty metres. This is the system I prefer for guided museum visits. The equipment may be connected to the listener's hearing aid or, in the case of mildly or moderately deaf visitors, may be used with no hearing aid at all.

3 The infra-red system This works on the same principle, but the electro-magnetic wave is replaced by a light wave. When someone speaks this produces a flux. A carrier provides for frequency modulation, exactly as on a radio set, and the sound is transmitted by diode; the signal – which will not be perceived by the eye because it is infra-red – is picked up by the receiver diode, demodulated and passed on either to earphones or to a small and less conspicuous device. As in the case of the high-frequency equipment, there is a wide range of possibilities, as the system is extremely adaptable.

Each system has its advantages and drawbacks. Two I feel to be particularly well suited to museum visits – the guided visit in which the guide-lecturer speaks and moves about and may be accompanied on his 'travel' by visitors with impaired hearing. The infra-red system is generally a fixture and it is very difficult to use it when moving about. If you have fifty rooms to take your visitors through I would therefore rather recommend the high-frequency system. If, on the contrary, you wish to receive groups of visitors not all of whom are deaf the infra-red equipment is preferable. For example, you can turn on a tape-recorder inside a room and the listener's movements will be determined by what the tape says. Here there are several different possibilities: it will suffice to change the tape to obtain a spoken text in, say, English or German. The system is thus extremely adaptable and may be used not merely by those with defective hearing but by the rest of the visitors as well, whether French or otherwise, at a relatively low cost considering the potentialities. An HF system for twenty people costs about thirty thousand francs and a museum will require between ten and twenty such systems. An individual system with six transmitters costs between thirty and forty thousand francs. To wire a big hall seating from one to two thousand may cost as much as four or five hundred thousand francs.

If one is to equip a museum and wishes to choose the technically and financially most suitable arrangement one must first be familiar with every one of the elements.

Reception services for the deaf at the Cité des Sciences et de l'Industrie at La Villette in Paris

Guy Bouchauveau

I was born stone deaf, of parents with normal hearing, and I would like to begin by telling you about the way the deaf spend their leisure time. It must be realized that in most cases deaf people are isolated at work from the people around them who can hear. Even if they manage fairly well to express themselves orally, their conversations with their colleagues, however hard they try, are often superficial or even non-existent. They have few friends at work and little conversation during their working day. They thus have an enormous need at weekends to meet other deaf people and gossip with people who share their language and their culture. Their favourite spare-time occupations are therefore meetings with deaf people in their community centres and their sports clubs or at deaf people's communal dinners, where their hunger for communication and for expression in the sign language may be satisfied, frequently to the neglect of meetings with their families. In contrast it is very rare for them to visit a museum, attend a lecture or take part in other cultural activities, owing to the absence of provision for the sign language.

Five years ago guided visits with simultaneous interpretation in the French sign language began to be organized in various Paris museums. I was delighted when I heard the news, believing that the solution was the correct one and that I was at last going to be able to understand the lecturer. But when I arrived on the spot I was a bit disappointed: it is excellent that there are interpreters, but the lecturer, who can hear, remains what he or she is, with a culture and rhythm which are different from those of the deaf. I have difficulty in asking questions of such a person, and using an interpreter necessarily creates an indirect relationship which is not plain sailing.

At that stage I was invited to sit on a committee which was meeting once a month on the question of the accessibility of the future science and technology museum at La Villette. Here it became obvious that for the place to be accessible to the deaf there must necessarily be a deaf member on the staff; scientific knowledge could be passed on only by a deaf person able to adapt himself to the different language levels of the deaf community.

The committee finally drew up a charter; but when the Cité des Sciences et de l'Industrie was opened not all the provisions of this had been met. If the work begun on the problem of accessibility was to be carried further there needed to be handicapped people on the spot. A particular requirement of the charter had been the subtitling of the audio-visual programmes on show in the free areas, primarily for the benefit of deaf visitors; yet subtitles were practically non-existent. It had also been pointed out in the charter that there must be projectors to light up the interpreter in the cinemas, and nothing had been done about this either. However, the main requirement for the deaf had been satisfied, for a deaf member of staff had been taken on.

I was thus engaged at the Cité des Sciences et de l'Industrie in February 1986. To start with I needed to acquire a sound training in astronomy, geology and related subjects. The training course, which I am continuing to take, is translated in its entirety into the sign language by the Cité interpreter.

After I had been through a period of training, the first activities employing the sign language took place and the reactions of the deaf public were immediately found to be most interesting. The groups of deaf pupils who had come with their non-deaf teachers showed themselves to be extremely lively and asked an enormous number of questions, to the great surprise of their teachers who in class had found them 'passive'. Teachers regularly find in the course of such visits that their pupils know far more than they imagined and are well able to understand the scientific explanations, and that some among them who have previously been classed as 'poor learners' owing to their lack of oral ability turn out to be lively and clever when they express themselves with the person of a deaf adult, and astounded that it should be possible to find a job even without speaking very well orally.

The 'Villette Classes' – held for two weeks at the Cité for the advanced study of a given subject – are extremely popular; the pupils are delighted and very often balk at returning to their ordinary school!

Non-deaf parents accompanying a deaf child are surprised to see how long their child is able to concentrate – sometimes for as much as two hours – when the lecturer is deaf and expresses himself in the sign language. Deaf adults are enthusiastic: at last they can venture to question the lecturer without fear of being taken for idiots, and their reactions show how important it is for the guide-lecturer to be deaf too. An elderly deaf man told us: 'I've had to wait twenty years to set foot in a museum and understand what was going on there!'

La Villette receives a great many foreign deaf visitors – Irish, Finnish, American, Argentinian, etc.: unlike those who can hear we have no need of interpreters.

One may also find deaf parents who have come with their non-handicapped children and feel embarrassed at using the sign language in public. When they see the guide-lecturer expressing himself quite naturally in the sign language, they discover that it is a beautiful language of which there is no need to be ashamed. Their visit to the Cité is often a revelation and a solace.

Frequently it happens that the hearing public, on seeing the deaf guide-lecturer, begins to feel curiosity about the sign language. The fact that it should be in use in a public place such as the Cité provides an excellent means of securing its recognition and enabling more to be known about it.

All of these reactions go to show how very positive are the net results of the use of the sign language as a medium for receiving museum visitors. The deaf public is enthusiastic, and it is also interesting to note the repercussions on the hearing public, which thus becomes accustomed to seeing the language used by those around them.

It should further be pointed out that at La Villette steps have been systematically taken to make the rest of the staff alive to what is involved. For this purpose I have run some non-verbal communication workshops, not for the study of the sign language but rather as an introductory measure, the idea being to do away with the feeling of fear often experienced by people who can hear when they meet deaf people for the first time.

I hope that in the near future an increasing number of museums will follow the example set at La Villette and that the deaf public will thus at long last have access through the sign language to the world of culture.

International Visual Art for the Deaf

Béatrice Derycke

International Visual Art for the Deaf is a very young association, not merely because it was only set up on 21 June 1989, but also – and primarily – because the average age of its officers and members is only thirty. Its youthfulness perhaps explains the dynamic way in which it is run.

It was on the association's initiative that the Direction des Musées de France and the Louvre together instituted a programme for the teaching of the history of art to the deaf. Deaf students are to be given a three-year training course, with annual exams, the purpose of which is to enable them to pass on their knowledge in the sign language directly to other deaf people, whether French or otherwise.

This system of direct communication is extremely important. Deaf adults will thus be enabled to follow what is being said about a work of art while looking at it, without the break in continuity caused by interpretation, and while appreciating all the subtle shades of expression of the sign language, which will be the lecturer's normal form of expression. It will also give them the possibility of communicating directly with the lecturer, through questions and answers.

For children it is also most important, since it will place the deaf children face to face with a deaf adult appearing as a highly qualified person (instead of the usual non-deaf adult), and will enable them to conceive of the possibility of acquiring the same sort of knowledge themselves.

The training is being arranged in close co-operation with the lecturers of the French national museums. The first ten students are highly motivated and fully conscious of the importance of their task. This will consist of giving deaf people readier access to museums, and so helping them to find their place in the world of culture in general, while also furthering the development of the language and culture of the deaf, notably through the finding or invention of new signs suited to the expression of abstract notions in art. It will also consist in encouraging the development of the culture of the deaf through contacts with other countries.

VI
Museums and mentally disabled people

Art and museums even for those who suffer the worst disadvantage

Jean de Ponthieu

The imperatives to be met if authentic initiation into culture is to be achieved include, side by side with the rest of the educational disciplines, effective training in creativeness and contact with original works. In this respect views on the mentally deficient sector of the most handicapped part of our society tend to vary.

Should educational efforts of this sort be envisaged for those who have difficulty even in adapting themselves to practical life? To reply in the negative would imply a disrespect for the rights of the individual which would be utterly scandalous. Yet this is often the case. How are we to explain it?

It might be said that embarrassment, rejection or hasty creationist and conservative ways of conceiving of the problem do harm to us all and *a fortiori* to those directly concerned. Such attitudes derive from unreasonable fears or from cut-and-dried formulae which may be combated by anyone able to question or to reflect on what he has been told. There is so great a misunderstanding of the phenomena of failure to adapt that the initiatives aimed at the elucidation of the data we at present possess on the subject can never be sufficient in number.

What does the expression 'mentally handicapped' actually cover?

We are not going here to undertake a fresh study of the mental handicap or of mental disorders; we shall merely be providing a few specific facts for the benefit of those who are asking themselves questions about the admission of the mentally deficient to places where works of art may be regularly seen. It would appear legitimate for the desire of such persons for access to the world to be encouraged by the provision of information, which, though certainly not exhaustive, may be capable of satisfying their initial expectation.

Many people will feel that it is obviously a matter of intelligence. But what is intelligence?

'Intelligence is what my test serves to measure.' This facetious retort ascribed to Alfred Binet is famous. Far from being an incitement to distribute intelligence quotients in the light of the results of the tests, it is a warning to the convinced psychometrists. It deprives the word 'intelligence' of any objective significance in isolation from the test itself. Moreover, the attempts based on different conceptions to separate intelligence from a given cultural context so as to arrive at a 'pure intelligence' would not appear any more convincing either.

The different types of mental handicap

Even if we agree to conceive of the development of children or adults as a process calling on a certain endowment with multiple and variable potentialities, there is no denying that the difficulties born of the initial structures of that endowment may constitute a mental handicap.

There is a very small percentage of cases of grave mental deficiency due to organic causes affecting the working of the brain. The chromosomal abnormalities causing trisomy are well known too; but this in no way means that all trisomics are fated to undergo identical intellectual development.

Most cases of moderate mental deficiency cannot be considered as genetic in origin. Hence in all these cases, as in the milder ones, and as in all cases of retarded development, the causes must be sought for in the dialectic of relations with the milieu in the broadest sense of that term. It is here that the analysts will encounter the difficulties to be overcome and the sources of the internal conflicts.

Under the traditional conception of the structural aspect of deficiency pride of place was given to ordinary harmonic deficiency, mainly showing itself in intellectual backwardness. The other forms of progressively worsening and disharmonic deficiency were considered merely as complications of this, aggravated further by disorders appearing to be separate and considered as 'associated'. The present-day position is that what were claimed to be complications are inherent in the structures themselves.

The development of the personality

It is an abusive practice to classify intellectual retardation in terms of IQ. But the psychometric approach dies hard, and has produced an official classification under the headings of mild deficiency (with a polite suggestion of subnormality), moderate deficiency, grave deficiency and moronism. Yet one may note the existence of differing degrees of intellectual ability during practical training, in behaviour and in relations with other people.

Longitudinal research has revealed an extreme clinical polymorphism in the initial structure and in the actual progress of the condition. Basically the development of the personality of a mentally handicapped person takes place along exactly the same lines as that of the person classed as normal: it will be dependent on the extent to which the internal conflicts have been settled. The personality gradually takes shape; it is not ready-made at the outset. Its structure will be determined dialectically in the social context within which the history of the individual concerned takes its course. The endowment is constantly involved, but it is not something immutable bestowed once and for all. Its nature may appear to differ according to situation. It represents at any given moment the means which the individual has available for dealing with the situation with which he is confronted at that moment.

These factors clearly signify that such notions as feeblemindedness, disability or normality have only a relative value. Since 'everything' must be taken into account it will be easy to imagine the importance of the way in which the handicapped person is viewed by the outsider. This last remark perhaps applies more strongly than the rest to the mentally handicapped who have been in institutions and are in many cases readmitted into society only in successive stages.

In reply to the sceptics who are convinced that mental deficiency is irrevocable and behavioural abnormality an irreversible fact, we may point out that stable normality is no more than a myth.

To those who find rigid classification reassuring we cannot too warmly recommend the reading of Tony Lainé's *Le Petit Donneur d'Offrandes*, which shows how far the disorders of mentally defective patients are the outcome of the hazards of their personal history. Yet their history could be that of persons considered to be normal.

The frontiers separating adaptation from failure to adapt are fragile and are as conventional as those frontiers which have poisoned the history of the world.

Receiving the mentally handicapped

In practice the task of the specialized institutions already includes accepting those who are 'different' with all their current differences and making them authentically welcome. Ability to achieve this is the result of a permanent effort to arrive at the best sort of relations within the community. To begin with this implies the building-up of an essential activity which is at least as important as the technical side of the task.

Such institutions, if they are to be consistent with themselves, must necessarily be in genuine touch with the world; all of them desire this and many of them achieve it. This desire for contact should receive a positive response from the public; but good intentions should not resolve themselves into the expert preparation of an over-protective system for receiving the comers. Staffs of museums and cultural bodies are capable, with the aid of escorts, of mingling know-how with sensitivity and making the right sort of carefully chosen arrangements to facilitate accessibility.

They may rest assured that to different degrees – as in the case of any visitor – they will be able to arouse pleasure in 'their' visitors, and to secure a degree of concentration which in reality will come more easily than in a conventional lesson. Educational benefit, too, even in the sense of the strict acquisition of knowledge, is not ruled out in a large number of cases.

The mentally handicapped and the work of art

How far is one to suppose that this public is genuinely interested in art? The tendency to consider that 'they don't understand' is highly significant. It reflects at once a misunderstanding of mental deficiency and a certain way of looking at art as such.

One must have lived in a specialized institution to be able to appreciate the extent to which its patients can be sensitive to their surroundings, provided only that they are encouraged to be so through attempts to comply with their wishes where these surroundings are concerned.

The research done on the less serious cases of deviation from the normal justify the belief that the mentally handicapped can be creative and can be receptive to the works of art. Appearances are against them, but motivation, the life impulse and the cultivation of their sensibility will prevail.

The initial contact with an original work of art during a visit to an exhibition will frequently cause utter delight. The reactions will be revealing: sculpture will be stroked in the direction of the grain, comments will be made on the painters' ability, satisfaction will be expressed with the colours or with the atmosphere of a picture.

It will be observed that the mentally handicapped, like children between the ages of two and eight, will be attracted by abstract works and by Fauvism; frequently the palm goes to Miró, Mondrian, de Staël or Matisse, and Chagall, or perhaps Dufy, also deserve special mention. But they may also have a special liking for the effects produced by such techniques as that of Seurat, for example.

It is quite obviously not a matter of absolute constants. An initiation through use of the active method at school will cause tastes to develop and will further broaden the field of motivations in the direction of a visual appetite. Pleasure is clearly experienced in the course of the actual creative activity, through painting and drawing using a variety of implements and processes. The different discoveries are reflected in surges of interest leading up to a pleasant state of excitement.

The part to be played

No one can be in any doubt as to the ability of curators to contribute to the formation of taste and to the provision of the pleasure of seeing and of the sensory encounter with the work of art. It is to be hoped that they will be prepared to commit themselves to the task of innovating in their work with the most severely deprived members of society.

Genuine lovers of art will be deeply convinced of the need for its popularization with everyone, including mentally handicapped children and adults. The custodians passionately attached to the works in their keeping and the defenders of the artistic heritage must step up their initiatives and place themselves at the head of the movement together with the teachers and educators. They will thus be further pursuing the work of the artist in ensuring the vitality and widespread influence of art as something which cannot be treated as a privilege for some and a vague and inaccessible goal for others.

In so doing they will be certain to earn the gratitude of the majority among us.

Museum programmes designed for mentally disabled visitors

Charles K. Steiner

I once took a field trip to a museum, an 'outdoor' museum. I was the director of a summer residential vacation camp for mentally retarded children and adults: Camp Tapawingo, an American Indian word for 'Land of Peace and Joy'. I wanted the campers at Tapawingo to see a beautiful, very large African textile that was on exhibition at this nearby museum. This wonderful work, I hoped, would inspire the campers' own creativity in creating works of art back at camp. I made an appointment in advance for all 120 campers and staff to visit the museum on a particular day and time. Upon arriving, we were greeted by two ladies in white gloves who led us to a closed carnival tent, set aside from the facility's main structure. A young man played a guitar and sang American folk songs, while the ladies passed out peanut butter and jelly sandwiches. After thirty minutes the ladies thanked me for coming and suggested that we return to our buses. The only trouble was that we hadn't come to the museum for peanut butter and jelly sandwiches and to be serenaded with American folk songs. We had come to see the giant African textile and to attend a puppet show and, by that point, the group needed to use a WC. The ladies said that the textile area was closed, the puppet show was inappropriate for 'our audience' and that it would be better if we could wait and use the WC back at camp. I sent a staff member to scout the 'closed' building and he found it open. He also found the puppet show to be a musical comedy, perfect for the group. I led the campers, against the wishes of the white-gloved ladies, to see the textile and, then, to attend the puppet show. At the conclusion of the puppet show, we used the WC and returned to the buses.

This incident aptly illustrates the lack of understanding by an American museum for the mentally disabled visitor and, to some degree, the lack of my understanding as the director of a social agency for the mission of museums. Museums must open their doors to all the disabled, including the mentally handicapped, but the disabled, their families and attendant staff must also realize the missions of museums as preservers of heritage, and not daycare. I should never have been permitted to bring 120 people on a single museum visit; at that time, I didn't know any better.

The goals of Disabled Visitor Services at the Metropolitan Museum of Art between 1976–86 were developed from such experiences as taking Tapawingo campers to museums for cultural enrichment. The ultimate aim of the programme, from its inception as 'Museum Education for Retarded Adults' in 1976 to the more diversified programme of later years, was to give disabled visitors first-hand contact with the collections side by side and equal to that experienced by the general public. This is not to say that it was easy initially to fund these programmes. I secured one grant – that included my salary – which in turn provided a foundation for the next grant. Disabled Visitor Services at the Metropolitan stressed methods that could be utilized in the public galleries. For example, touching works of art was discouraged in favour of walking discussion groups where mentally disabled visitors learned appropriate museum behaviour while looking at art. This also aided in promoting repeated visits. Presumably, even if I could arrange for a mentally disabled person to touch an object, he or she couldn't return on a Saturday with family, without me, and expect the security guard to stand idly by while the visitor touched objects on exhibition. A visually impaired person might understand the distinction; a mentally retarded person, for example, does not.

To ensure that my museum experience with Camp Tapawingo would never happen at the Metropolitan, Disabled Visitor Services offered a package of education programmes, aimed at a broader audience than just the disabled visitor: for museum staff, the developmentally disabled visitor's chaperone and the general public. Orientation sessions were organized for social service personnel attending the disabled visitor in advance of the appointed visits. The format for orientation sessions included a highlights tour of the museum, focusing on a number of the great masterpieces in the collection. Also included was general information pertaining to the accessibility of the museum. These sessions demonstrated that the Metropolitan Museum cared a great deal about the mentally retarded or the learning disabled and the accompanying staff. It also served to identify a museum contact person in a large institution where telephone calls can often be lost or put on indefinite 'hold'. In order for these programmes to succeed, it was essential for the museum to return support to the social agency. To this end, I worked to lend the name of the Metropolitan to area social agency by attending art shows at such places as the Lighthouse for the Blind, serving on the voluntary curatorial art board of a hospital and generally taking every opportunity to encourage art programming in the community and to help social agency staff who supported the museum's programme. For example, works of art selected by the Art Board were shown in the psychiatric corridors of Bellevue Hospital in New York.

Training Metropolitan Museum staff to be as receptive and gracious to the disabled, including the mentally disabled, as they were to other visitors was difficult. I had little trouble organizing training sessions on disability for staff who ranked below me. I had a lot of trouble educating staff who ranked above me – department heads, curators and administrators. Most successful was identifying colleagues who were sympathetic to the cause and then encouraging them to educate *their* own colleagues. Distinguished staff from the museum world, such as a curator of British painting from Yale University, toured disabled visitors, including the mentally disabled, through the gallery and then reported this experience to problematic Metropolitan Museum colleagues. Contributing to the programme was the personnel development of my own junior colleagues, who, in ten years, rose through the ranks of the museum from relatively unimportant jobs to positions of influence. Having been won over to the programme in the early years, they were now in a position to legislate a great deal of support through the personnel and financial structures of the museum.

I've discussed educating social agency and museum staff to the special needs of mentally disabled visitors, but what teaching techniques are most effective in working with the mentally disabled themselves? I learned at Camp Tapawingo that an essential teaching method in special education is repetition. To this end, the Metropolitan's programmes were designed to ensure opportunities for reinforcement by discouraging one-time only visits. If a teacher could reinforce in a classroom, why shouldn't the museum have the same opportunity? A chaperone was required to guarantee that the same group would return to the museum more than once, and that the same group would be available for a pre-visit slide show in advance of the museum visit. These programmes were extremely successful and are outlined in detail in the technical assistance manuals available by mail-order through the Metropolitan. For example, one particularly excellent programme, organized with the New York Association for the Help of Retarded Citizens, structured a programme of visits alternating between the art museum and a sculpture studio. One group's first assignment was to build a ceramic tower, based on the previous week's museum study of fundamental composition and shapes involving intriguing museum objects like a nineteenth-century Javanese xylophone. A different group from another social agency looked at paintings with similarly encouraging results.

Despite the emphasis on programming in the museum's galleries, there remained a great number of disabled people isolated in hospitals and residential facilities who never have the opportunity to go to the Metropolitan, or any other museum. Disabled Visitor Services organized small exhibitions, like the one entitled 'Picture of Medieval Life', that took works of art to hospital lobbies, among other places, in an effort to reach this population. The exhibitions were small – as few as twenty objects, and security risks required that cases sometimes looked more like armoured tanks than museum vitrines, but the shows served an enormous audience.

Except for the travelling exhibitions, these programmes were all taking place in the public galleries of the Metropolitan and, thus, it was important to educate the general public. If a mother suddenly clutches her baby as a disabled group walks by, or a member of the general public sends some other similar signal of discomfort, the museum education programme has been irreversibly undercut. It is difficult enough for those of us with normal capacities to overcome such rudeness and refocus on the mentally disabled. How do we reach an amorphous group like the general museum-visiting public? The answer: by raising the programme's profile and by building an association between the museum and the disabled in the minds of the public so that visitors almost anticipate sharing the galleries with disabled people. Publications promoting access for disabled visitors were distributed at the Information Desk in the Great Hall of the museum alongside other museum publications. Blockbuster exhibitions included special large-type publications for the blind prominently displayed; the museum's regular maps and guides were integrated with handicap-related information – the location of the accessible rest-room, the telephone for the deaf and the telephone numbers where a visitor could reach additional information. To increase their appeal to any visitor, the publications focused on the chief interest of the general visiting public: works of art. A brochure on the mentally retarded or a programme for families with a disabled family member featured a work of art on its cover, not a wheelchair and not a picture of cute disabled children smiling.

I could not close without acknowledgement that Disabled Visitor Services at the Metropolitan continue today under the capable leadership of someone else. I had reached a point with the programme where it risked taking on my personality rather than a life of its own governed by the needs of its constituents. There was also the issue of whether such a programme would be better directed by a disabled person; after all, it no longer served just mentally disabled people but all potential disabled visitors. I had grown weary, too, of fighting the noble battle of museum education and was anxious to see if I could not provide more support for programmes like Disabled Visitor Services and museum education in general if I were a museum administrator – a position I now hold as Assistant Director of the Art Museum at Princeton University.

Museums and mentally disabled people

I am ambitious for museum education and I am ambitious for the disabled museum visitors, including the mentally disabled visitors; but, once again, a partnership is needed. We, as museum personnel, must bestow a dignity on the profession of museum education, which, some fifteen years after my problems with the white-gloved ladies, it still lacks. The social agencies, special education teachers and advocates for the mentally disabled must raise their goals and not crumble so easily with the day-to-day fatigue and frustrations in caring for mentally disabled people.

Ultimately we all stand to gain, with a considerable improvement in quality of life: the mentally disabled with a large number of cultural choices and increased likelihood of reaching full educational potential; the museum profession, with a more diverse audience and a greater understanding of our fellow citizens, especially the understanding that visual appreciation does not necessarily go hand in hand with intellectual acuity.

The National Museum of Fine Arts in Karlsruhe, Germany

Gert Reising

In addition to its Dutch, French and German sections the National Museum of Fine Arts in Karlsruhe has since the late 1950s had a museum education service, and since the 1970s it has had a children's museum.

The aim of those in charge is social and aesthetic familiarity with art. The aids at their disposal are a slide library, a painting studio and the possibility of arranging lectures, advanced training and programmes for all levels, from primary school to adult education classes.

Visitors come from Karlsruhe and the surrounding area, and just under half of the annual total of 130,000–150,000 are catered for by the education services, which provide programmes for backward children, visually handicapped people, war-blinded and the mentally handicapped.

Up to now we have run five courses for the mentally handicapped, four of which were for schoolchildren. One such course lasted seven years altogether, though another was interrupted on the grounds that it was 'pornographic': a picture representing nudes had been used. Since the early 1980s a course for a group of live-in workers from one of the Hagsfelder Workshops in Karlsruhe – a sheltered workshop – has been regularly held at the museum, with classes once a week.

The work with the mentally handicapped serves the specific purpose of breaking down the barriers between one student and another and encouraging their integration into the life of an 'open' society. No therapeutic purpose is intended.

In 1982 the paintings of the schoolchildren were shown at an exhibition, and a further one for adult work is scheduled for 1991. But despite wide publicity on the media the exhibition had only a mild success. We proposed further courses, but scarcely anyone showed interest.

Museums and mentally disabled people

One group of mentally handicapped young people between the ages of twelve and twenty took part in a regular activity at the museum for seven years. It all started when a woman member of the staff caring for them boldly asked for a guided visit to our gallery to be arranged. We rapidly came to an agreement on the idea of devising a course: we had good pictures and possessed a painting studio, and we felt that painting and looking at pictures could be associated activities.

We felt there would be problems in that we would be offering 'only' paintings and sculptures, affording no practical interest beyond progress in painting and modelling. But it turned out that in works of art we found sufficient subjects possessed of significance for the students.

Few of those attending the course had a basic physical handicap: all were capable of receiving a 'practical' education. We shared experiences which reflected themselves in the subsequent behaviour of the students in the presence of strangers and in an institution foreign to them. We attached greater importance to their relations with each other and with the museum than to the pictures they produced and to our own paintings. The pictures are rather to be seen as a record of their intercourse with each other and with art. This does not mean that aesthetic enjoyment was ruled out.

The mentally handicapped always remain cut off from the rest of us. There was, it is true, in 1981, which was the International Year of Disabled Persons, a special issue of *Kunst und Unterricht* for the occasion (No. 69), but no single article was devoted to the mentally handicapped. Yet it is this isolation which certainly causes the largest number of problems. It became clear to me that the students taking the course were becoming less and less retarded. The reason was a growing sense of security on their part, together with a decrease in my nervousness at being with them.

We were communicating on the subject of the works of art, all of which provided a necessary impetus. But the interest aroused by the aesthetic aspect came only second or third. The museum offered only what, as a museum, it was able to do, i.e. pictures to be looked at. Provision was necessarily made for the needs of the students, and any idea of treatment was left aside. Treatment is the affair of specialists who are as knowledgeable in respect of the pictorial images in the minds of their patients as in respect of their art, and know how to make their assessments. Such a task would have involved us in too many risks from both points of view. We therefore confined ourselves to making use of pictures which were accessible, and could be examined in the light of the rules, through analysis of their execution, raising, for example, questions of perspective or angle of vision.

When we commented together on the pictures we discussed the possibilities of achieving intelligible results in painting. But such assessment we found the more difficult in that our own conception of form and rule is distinct from that of the people who themselves produce works of art and from that of the mentally handicapped who draw and paint. In both these groups there is the same clearly expressed violation of accepted forms and rules. What is sought to express will differ, and prudence is called for. There have been enough attempts to pit art and normality against mental deficiency and narrow-mindedness. The question is: whose normality, and whose is the greater risk? We have kept as far away from the theory of therapy through art as from a rejection of psychiatry. We also try to take into account the rules governing perspective and changes of direction from right to left or vice versa and to discover how far they can serve to set standards.

For us, those we work with are handicapped and it is our sense of objectivity which must dominate. There are no 'ifs' and 'buts'; for us the negation of the bourgeois rules of perspective by Michael W. is every bit as interesting as their negation by Joan Miró.

But what is certain at all events is that our starting point was neither the therapeutic aspect – for the educator – nor the artistic one, as museum people. We were interested neither in the Prinzhorn Collection and Leo Navratil's definition of art (see, for example, *Kunst jenseits der Kunst* in the exhibition catalogue of the Wedding Art Institute, Berlin, 1980), nor in the unusual case (Gaston Chaissac or Friedrich Schröder-Sonnenstern, Michael W. or Ingrid R.). What we were concerned with was presenting processes and observing progress of which young people held to be abnormal were capable.

Perhaps the only measurable result is that for both the adolescents and the adults intercourse with strangers, with art and with their own creative potentialities has become easier. Still further integration would be a help to them. For us it has never been a question of curative treatment.

Each visit to the museum takes place roughly as follows:

1. The group chooses a painting from the collection in the museum. The choice, initially made by me alone, was determined by problems of form (e.g. the manner of representing standing, sitting or recumbent figures and groups, the composition with or without perspective and the colour scheme), and also by the intended content (communication, dancing, relations between members of society, relations with places, group activity, the seasons, dreams, inner experience, etc.). At the present time the groups walk through the collections and choose a picture for them-

selves. Care is taken, however, to see that a given subject does not recur too often (still lifes, for instance, tend to do so, notwithstanding the problems of composition involved).

2. The group comments on the work for a quarter of an hour, explains the picture, links its subject with personal associations and chats informally about it. We do our best to see that such discussion is as far as possible run independently by the group (with no 'art history guidance'). The discussions are designed to improve the young students' ability to associate with people, since most of them are rather shy and will not start a conversation on their own initiative.

3. Sometimes, if there are too many details or the picture presents too many difficulties, the subject will first be sketched. Pencil and paper will permit a spontaneous and lively stylization which will fill the sheet, with no thought of colour. This will demand about five minutes, rarely longer. Everyone, including the accompanying staff, will do the drawing.

4. The group paints the subject in the painting studio. Everyone paints, and so do the staff. No importance is assigned to the accuracy of the copy. The painting takes just under half an hour; it is done with broad brushes and thick poster paint, using the three primary colours (red, blue and yellow), plus black and white, and also the secondary colours green and brown, which are provided ready mixed, though violet must be obtained by mixing if required. Colours are mixed on palettes without assistance. Subsequently all members of the group put away their painting materials unaided.

5. The paintings are placed in a row and each is explained by its author. Questions are asked about the differences between the new version and the original and about the reasons for them. The composition is discussed. All members of the group take part in this discussion, so that the students themselves distribute praise and blame amongst themselves.

An article in *Zeitschrift für Kunstpädagogik*, 1982, No. 6, pp. 54–7, reports on our work, which there is no intention of bringing to an end. The courses are continuing and in 1991 we shall be presenting our work through an exhibition.

Services for the mentally handicapped at the Royal Castle in Warsaw, Poland

Jan Daniel Artymowski

The Royal Castle in Warsaw is in many ways unique as a museum. What it has to display are almost exclusively historic interiors and it is one of the best of its kind in Poland. It is also one of the most outstanding of our historical monuments, and in a country where the past is considered to be very much an element of the present this is important. Formerly the main royal residence and the seat of the Parliament for over two centuries, the Royal Castle, totally destroyed in the last war and now rebuilt, is in many respects an incarnation of our history.

The castle attracts large numbers of visitors and not all who are anxious to visit it can be immediately admitted. The regular stream of tourists is handled by paid guides, but museum lessons and handicapped visitors are the responsibility of the Education Service. This unit consists of about twenty people, three of whom work full time for the disabled, though should the need arise many other members of staff can be called on to help.

The term 'handicapped' is given a broad interpretation at the castle. It covers the blind, the deaf, the mentally handicapped, the mentally diseased, the physically handicapped, the elderly (especially those living in institutions) and many groups generally described as 'socially maladjusted': juvenile delinquents from special schools, orphans from children's homes, alcoholics undergoing hospital treatment. Our team caters for practically all those groups which have recognizable special needs: for these we have guided tours, museum lessons and films and extra-mural programmes such as lectures and slide shows. All these activities are free of charge; but if any of the aforesaid groups decide to buy their tickets and hire a guide they will pay the normal fee.

The mentally retarded are frequent visitors to the Royal Castle. Like other visitors they can of course be divided into different categories, each of which will present the museum educator with specific problems of its own. There are the slightly retarded and the more gravely affected, the sighted retarded and the blind retarded ...

When working with these groups we face different kinds of problems, according to the type of handicap. One problem will always be that of communication – of expressing frequently complicated things in sufficiently simple language and in a dynamic enough way to arouse their interest.

The simplest form of service to the mentally handicapped visiting the castle is naturally the guided tour. This is the form generally adopted for groups coming from distant towns who are not likely to come again. Our overall aim is to make such tours pleasant and not overloaded; but we try to have a clear view of what we would like the group to remember. The tour covers two or three subjects repeated in different ways.

For schools from Warsaw and its environs we generally prefer to organize museum lessons, the subjects and the form of which depend on the age of the children and on their degree of handicap. Under our school system mentally handicapped children are generally divided in practice into two categories: the slightly handicapped go to what are known as 'special' schools, which are really simplified versions of the mainstream 'normal' school, but with a simplified syllabus, smaller classes, more sophisticated teaching methods, etc. Since rudiments of history are included in the Polish language classes, and since history is also taught as a separate subject, we try to adapt our lessons to the school syllabus. Thus the subjects proposed for museum lessons in the castle are 'Old Warsaw in Canaletto's Paintings', 'The King and his Coronation', 'Parliament' and 'The Constitution of the Third of May'. Other subjects may be chosen but are seldom requested by teachers, who have a tendency to remain somewhat passive.

In addition, when we are showing major historical exhibitions we use them as a basis for lessons prepared for the 'special' schools. These are generally very much in demand – far more so than our regular lessons, which are planned in the form of a series; it would appear to be much easier for the teachers to make a single effort than to co-operate with us systematically year after year. As we see it, the ideal situation would be for a class to attend all the lessons planned by the castle as they fit into the school syllabus, familiarizing themselves in the process with the castle interiors, with the history of Poland and with our own persons. Since, especially in the case of retarded children, learning is largely a matter of repetition, and since we are anxious to enter into some sort of personal relationship with the children, this would appear to be the best method.

Mentally handicapped at the Royal Castle, Warsaw

Our main problem in preparing these lessons is how to select the material. Generally we choose the few facts we want the children to remember and repeat them in different situations. We often introduce an element of play to make the lesson less monotonous. As an example of our method I will describe a lesson entitled 'The King and his Coronation'. This is preceded by a slide show and talk at the school, given by whoever is to serve as the guide at the castle. The aim of this is threefold: to learn as much as possible about the children, to allow them to get to know the guide so that when they come to the castle there will be at least one person there with whom they are acquainted and to prepare them for the subject to be presented during the visit. During the talk I generally show the children the main symbols of royal power, briefly discuss the coronation rites and explain the functions a king of Poland was expected to fulfil. In the castle a few days later the children have an opportunity of seeing many of the things they saw on slides and the same information is repeated in the royal chamber in front of busts, portraits, thrones, etc. After the visit we play at coronations and during the game a king is elected and a bishop is appointed to crown the king and the queen – whom the king chooses among much giggling. Other children also take part in the scene; there are more than enough roles to go round. Elements of historical costumes help to create the right atmosphere, and sometimes a film is shown at the end of the lesson, though the films we possess were not made specially for the purpose and are a bit too general. Nevertheless we frequently include one in the programme, since going to the castle cinema to see a film is considered to be one of the attractions of the visit.

We assume that the teachers repeat in class what was taught during the lesson. If they care to do so they can buy slides and brochures at the castle shop.

Lessons with more seriously retarded children, who go to what are called 'schools of life', present different problems. The purpose of these schools is to teach the children how to cope with the tasks of everyday life. Elements of history and cultural tradition – especially of a local nature – are included in the syllabus, so that co-operation with a museum such as ours is possible. Guided tours are feasible, of course; but with Warsaw schools we again endeavour to work in two successive series of lessons. The series comprises two or three talks illustrated by slides, followed by visits to the Castle, and is repeated after an interval of two years. The subjects include general historical topics, such as the king and how to recognize him, his family (with the titles given to his wife and children), elements of the castle's history (its destruction during the war and its post-war reconstruction) and its present-day functions.

However, the lessons have other purposes as well. The introduction of a stranger to the class, the presentation of colour slides and the visit to a new and beautiful place all help to arouse the children's interest in many simple things, which need not be specifically 'royal'. We have, for example, a whole lesson which consists in recognizing and naming different pieces of furniture and interior decoration, counting features seen in the rooms and also recognizing the different functions of the various interiors – all of them things which could, for the most part, probably be practised outside the castle but which are especially attractive and stimulating inside it. The children seem to be more keen in that unusual setting to learn and to use the knowledge they already possess. A repetition of the sequence two years later will reveal that the children have retained almost everything – a fact which does not cease to amaze me, since all other special groups tend to forget most of what they have learned very quickly.

The second series of talks and visits is designed to broaden the knowledge of the group a little, and to make what it already knows more operative. In addition to all this, I find working with the 'school of life' children very rewarding, as they are very warm and affectionate.

In lessons or guided tours with the deaf we use more or less the same methods, though the communication barrier seems to be greater than elsewhere. The vocabulary of an average deaf person in Poland is often very similar to that of a moderately retarded person, or in other words very poor. At the same time the deaf children have quite an ambitious school syllabus in history – and very poor memories. This sometimes compels us to try to explain very difficult things in very simple language.

The blind retarded children who come to the castle are generally only slightly retarded, and are handled in more or less the same way as the other children from special schools, except for the use of tactile methods.

To sum up, these lessons have, in our view, a threefold function. There is obviously the task of conveying information: we are trying to broaden our visitors' knowledge of history and art. Then there is the function of stimulation: we are trying to get them interested in what they see and hear. The unusual and beautiful surroundings inside the castle often serve to interest them in a great variety of things not necessarily directly connected with our subjects. And, last but not least, we consider that we have the task of making the handicapped feel really welcome and wanted, as unfortunately is rarely the case in our society. We consider that failure to achieve this would make our educational efforts worthless.

Personally I find working with the mentally retarded, as with the other handicapped groups, very rewarding. The problems which arise, especially with mentally retarded visitors, force us to rethink our methods of communication and this helps us to be more explicit with other people. It also obliges us to ask an important question: what is the important factor, the point of encounter with those we are guiding, those we called 'handicapped'? It will rarely be knowledge, since in general it is we who are the experts. It will rarely be the intellect – least of all in the case of those who belong to the category of the mentally handicapped. It must therefore be what we call the heart. A great deal is said about lifts, platforms, specially adapted lavatories and many other very necessary things which make buildings accessible. But it might be equally well to think of the lifts, staircases or platforms which will give access to our hearts. For it is in our hearts that all these barriers – technical, sociological and emotional – are born.

Hence before we begin to dismantle these barriers in our museums we should search our hearts. Perhaps then we will discover that there is not after all so great a difference between our handicapped clients and ourselves. For, if I may paraphrase a verse from St Paul, there is no difference at all: we are all handicapped and far away from God's saving presence. If we accept that as true we will not behave to the handicapped as rich to poor, clever to stupid and strong to weak. The truth is that we are all poor but we ourselves have something to share with others.

I feel that if we succeed in achieving this our entire attitude to our work and to our visitors, whether handicapped or not, can change. For me personally, working with the handicapped has led to the conclusion that they require the very best. To serve them properly requires a maximum physical, intellectual and emotional effort.

It was only after some time had elapsed that I discovered that other people require no less.

Afterword

Nancy Breitenbach

'Museums and Disabled People' was the first international conference on the theme, and the first international event organized by the Fondation de France. In initiating this movement forward, the Fondation de France had two major objectives: to draw public attention to a problem which few officials and professionals are aware of, and to encourage such persons to take action by providing examples of appropriate solutions.

In assembling over 250 people from the cultural and social spheres, representing many nations, 'Museums and Disabled People' reinforced the convictions of those who were already aware of the various obstacles met by the disabled, and enlightened others, mobilizing all to greater efforts so that museums may become more accessible in every way to people who have handicaps.

Such a positive response is gratifying. But it is well known that modifying general attitudes and transforming public buildings takes time, and progress could be expected to be slow. Has this been the case? Definitely not. In the space of one and a half years, significant steps have been taken.

Ground has been gained in two ways:

- official recognition of the problem by various authorities, and inclusion of the theme in their statements concerning cultural policy;
- concrete measures and specific actions, in France and abroad.

In France the situation has evolved quite positively. First of all, several initiatives have furthered the cause by promoting the principle of access to museums for the disabled. The publication of the second volume of the Fondation de France's *Cultural Guide to Paris* for people with handicaps, with its detailed section on museums, was well received. The national competition for museum services for the blind, organized jointly by the Valentin Haüy Association (AVH), the Fondation de France and the Direction des Musées de France (DMF), awarded prizes to three

Afterword

initiatives in 1989 (the Château de Blois in the Val de Loire, the Musée Picasso in Antibes and the travelling exhibition 'Tissus-Tact') and was renewed in 1990. A similar competition, covering services for people with developmental disabilities and organized by the National Union of Associations of Parents of Handicapped Children (UNAPEI) together with the DMF and the Fondation de France, was also launched in 1990.

Second, projects to adapt physical settings and establish long-term programmes have multiplied. The DMF has initiated specialized training for its personnel. The Greater Louvre, which opened its doors a few months after the 1988 conference, has provided an excellent illustration of how accessibility can be compatible with architectural aesthetics and museological practice, as well as how all museum visitors can profit from well-conceived services. The Fine Arts Museum in Rouen has incorporated the needs of the disabled into its renovation programme. The Musée en Herbe, a well-known children's museum in the Bois de Boulogne near Paris, is programming research so that *all* children may actively participate in the new permanent exhibit, 'Art in Europe', due to open in 1992. And many other museums are joining the movement: adapted facilities, special documentation in printed or recorded form, better staff awareness, etc.

Action has broadened to include access to historical monuments. In response to the request expressed by the Directorate of National Heritage and in co-operation with the National Board of Historical Monuments and Sites (CNMHS), the Fondation de France brought together a working committee composed of representatives of both organizations and competent specialists working in the field of disability. The sessions have resulted in new training possibilities for personnel concerned with visitor services and the beginnings of a census of historical monuments and sites in France which offer services meeting the needs of disabled persons; such information will be ultimately incorporated into the national guide published and distributed by the CNMHS, *Ouvert au public*.

These initiatives have been accompanied by local actions, such as the choice of 'The New Publics' as the theme for the 1990 International Meeting on Cultural Heritage, organized in Avignon. Exactly two years after organizing its conference in Unesco House in Paris, the Fondation de France will be actively supporting a new conference, intended, once again, to promote better services for disabled visitors to the thousands of historical buildings in France.

Such efforts require financial as well as moral investment, and it has been gratifying to remark that since November 1988, the call for 'access to culture and the arts' has obtained response from the private as well as the public sector. Following the example set by the Fondation Otis, a number of new corporate partners have selected this theme for their sponsorship programmes.

The cry for better museum services for disabled persons is heard far beyond France's borders. In preparing this book, the Fondation de France and ICOM have had the opportunity to collect information on a number of initiatives across the continent, and to draw on these experiences in order to enrich the book's contents. Meetings and conferences have been organized in several countries, with objectives concurrent with those of the Paris conference: inform the decision- and policy-makers of the needs of the disabled visitors to museums and suggest possible solutions. Among these events, an Italian session conducted in 1989 and the Glasgow (UK) conference on 'Art Horizons 1990' have been of particular interest.

But so much remains to be done, in so many settings throughout Europe and around the world! Ready access for disabled people to the riches available in numberless cultural sites – places filled with knowledge, history and tradition – is a necessity which has little to do with national boundaries. The fact that the problem is international is one of the reasons for publishing this book in two language versions, French and English. The message must be spread as far as possible.

This book ends with the same strong affirmation as that which was pronounced at its beginning – *culture is not a luxury*, it is an essential link between the members of a community. In Europe and elsewhere, disabled people must have the opportunity to share our common cultural heritage. Only in this way will they be truly full members of society.

Select bibliography

This bibliography has been compiled by Emmanuelle Eskenazi for the UNESCO–ICOM Information Centre and refers to select documents concerning museums as they relate to the disabled: books, periodical articles, proceedings of conferences and seminars since 1965. Main references are followed by a short abstract.

It updates and expands the bibliography compiled by Anne Raffin in October 1988 from the collections of the ICOM Information Centre in collaboration with the Fondation de France, the Direction des Musées de France and the Royal National Institute for the Blind. Searches were carried out on the main centres and associations for disabled people in France and in Europe.

I Cultural policies concerning disabled people, in France and abroad

Access to cultural opportunities. Museums and the handicapped. *Proceedings of the February 22-24, 1979 Conference* ... Washington, Association of Science–Technology Centers, 1980, viii, 189 pp., illus.

> Presenting the results of a conference convened with support of the National Endowment for the Arts and the Bureau of Education for Handicapped, this publication acquaints museum professionals with federal regulations on accessibility. Various viewpoints are considered: the architect's, the legislator's, educator's for handicapped people, museum personnel etc. Appendix I presents the Section 504 Regulations passed by the US Congress in September 1973, which prohibit discrimination on the basis of physical or mental handicap in every federal assisted programme in the USA.

After Attenborough: Arts and disabled people. London, Bedford Square Press [for] Carnegie United Kingdom Trust, 1988, ix, 122 pp., illus.

Arts and Disabled People. Report of Committee of Inquiry under the chairmanship of Sir Richard Attenborough. London, Bedford Square Press/NCVO for Carnegie United Kingdom Trust, 1985, xvii, 158 pp., illus.

> Results of an inquiry carried out by a committee appointed by the Carnegie UK Trust. Various ways of making the arts more accessible to disabled people are discussed, as well as the training of the staff. Useful addresses and recommendations are given in annex.

Arts and the Handicapped. An issue of access. A report from Educational Facilities Laboratories and the National Endowment for the Arts, New York, Educational Facilities Laboratories, 1975, 79 pp., illus.

Artymowsky, Daniel, A calling and a challenge: working for the handicapped at the Royal Castle in Warsaw. (*The International Journal of Museum Management and Curatorship*, Guildford, Vol. 5, No. 2, 1986, pp. 159–62, illus.)

Avan, Louis, Charte des personnes handicapées dans le musée national des

Select bibliography

sciences, des techniques et des industries de la Villette. (*Les études du musée national des sciences, des techniques et des industries*, Paris, No. 8, 1984, 116 pp., illus.)

A 'charter for the disabled', containing the various recommendations concerning physical and intellectual accessibility drawn up by a working group whose members included representatives of the non-museum world. It is a combination of different charters governing individual categories of disabled persons: the visually handicapped, the deaf and hard of hearing, the mentally handicapped, persons with walking difficulties, those with unapparent disabilities and those with multiple handicaps.

Avan, Louis, *La place des personnes handicapées au Musée de la Villette*. Paris, Cité des sciences et de l'industrie de la Villette, 1985, 7 pp., illus.

After an introduction to the museum in terms of figures, the author sums up the results of the 'Janus I' operation, during which several groups of disabled persons were taken round the museum. Accessibility is discussed from a theoretical and practical point of view and as an objective to be achieved via appropriate training of reception staff.

Bardt-Pellerin, Elisabeth, An experiment: guiding handicapped children in the museum. (*Gazette*, Ottawa, Vol. 14, Nos 1–2, 1981, pp. 18–30, illus., bibliogr.)

Barrier free. Positive steps to help the disabled. (*AGMANZ News*, Wellington, Vol. 12, No. 2, 1981, pp. 14–16.)

Callow, Kathy B., Museums and the disabled. (*Museums Journal*, London, Vol. 74, No. 2, 1974, pp. 70–2.)

Cook, Allison D., New York City's Community Art Resource for disabled persons. (*New York Community Art Resource*, New York, Vol. 3, No. 387, Dec. 1984.)

Dispelling myths opens museum to the disabled. (*ASTC Newsletter*, Washington, Vol. 8, No. 6, Nov.–Dec. 1980, p. 12.)

Fina, Kurt, Museum und Landschaft–Erleben, Lernen, Bildung. (*Museumskunde*, Frankfurt a.M., Vol. 45, No. 2, 1980, p. 52.)

Gall, Günter and Graf, Bernhard, Zur Situation der Behinderten im Museum. (*Museumskunde*, Frankfurt a.M., Vol. 47, No. 1, 1982, pp. 5-11.)

Gosling, D., Disabled visitors. (In *The Design of Educational Exhibits*, compiled by R. S. Miles, in collaboration with M. B. Alt, D. C. Gosling, B. N. Lewis and A. F. Tout. London, George Allen & Unwin, 1982, pp. 102–5, illus.)

Grandjean, Gilles, Musées et handicapés. Paris, Direction des Musées de France, Service d'Action Culturelle, 1986, 5 pp.

Heath, Alison M., Handicapped students and museums. (In *Museum Education Training. A conference of the Museum Education Association of Australia*, Sydney, NSW, Apr. 1977, pp. 19–23, illus.)

Heath, Alison M., The same only more so: museums and the handicapped visitor. (*Museums Journal*, London, Vol. 7, No. 2, 1976, pp. 56–8.)

Heer, Maria, Mitmachen möchte ich wohl … (*Neues Rheinland*, Pulheim, Vol. 32, No. 6, 1989 [n.p.].)

Help for the Special Educator: Taking a field trip to the Metropolitan Museum of Art. New York, The Metropolitan Museum of Art, 1981 40 pp., illus.

Inglis, Robin R., Editorial: Museums and the handicapped. (*Gazette*, Ottawa, Vol. 11, No. 3, 1978, pp. 2–6.)

James, Marianna S., One step at a time. How Winterthur approaches program accessibility. (*History News*, Nashville, Vol. 36, No. 7, 1981 pp. 10–15, illus.)

Keen, Carolyn, Visitor services and people with a disability. (*Museums Journal*, London, Vol. 84, No. 1, 1984, pp. 33–8, illus.)

Kelly, Elisabeth, New services for the disabled in American museums. (*Museums Journal*, London, Vol. 82, No. 3, 1982, pp. 157–9, illus.)

Kenney, Alice P., A test of barrier-free design. (*Museum News*, Washington, Vol. 55, No. 3, 1977, pp. 27–9, illus.)

Kunst und Behinderte. Clemens-Sels-Museum Dokumentation Symposion, Neuss, 1989 [n.p.

evette, Gina, *The Creative Tree: Active articipation in the arts for people who are isadvantaged*. Salisbury, Michael Russell ub., 1987, 296 pp., illus., bibliogr.

ühning, Arnold, Geistig Behinderte im 1useum. (*Museumskunde*, Frankfurt a.M., ol. 47, No. 1, 1982, pp. 5–11, illus.)

undström, Inga, Handicappade på museer. *Svenska museer*, Stockholm, No. 3, 1980, pp. 1–3, illus.)

1adden, Joan C., Joining forces. Reaching out ɔ special audiences. (*Museum News*, Vashington, Vol. 60, No. 4, 1982, pp. 38–41, lus.)

1ajewski, Janice, *Part of your General Public Disabled. A handbook for guides in useums, zoos and historic houses*. Vashington, Smithsonian Institution [for] Office of Elementary and Secondary ducation, 1987, 83 pp. [plus videotape; nanual also available in audio cassette and raille format].
Practical guide designed to raise the awareness of museum personnel and to offer solutions to problems faced by disabled visitors. From providing extensive descriptions of objects for visually handicapped people, to speaking clearly and directly to a hearing-impaired tour member, or presenting information simply and logically to a mentally retarded person, the manual outlines a range of practical ways in which docents, tour guides and others can help disabled people. The videotape shows individuals with different disabilities participating in tours in various museum settings.

1cLeod, Janette, Taking the inside out – an utreach programme for special groups. *Kalori*, Sydney, No. 50–60, 1982, pp. 74–6.)

1olloy, Larry, The case for accessibility. *Museum News*, Washington, Vol. 55, No. 3, 977, pp. 15–17, illus.)

1olloy, Larry, 504 Regs: learning to live by he rules. (*Museum News*, Washington, Vol. 7, No. 1, 1978, pp. 28–33.)

1olloy, Larry, Museum accessibility: the ontinuing dialogue. (*Museum News*, Vashington, Vol. 60, No. 2, 1981, pp. 50–7, lus.)

Monnin, B., Les musées et les personnes handicapées. (*Bonjour la vie*, Paris, Anpitim, No. 171, 1989, pp. 30–1.)

Monsieur Jack Lang veut encourager l'insertion des handicapés dans la vie culturelle. C.B. (*Le Monde*, Paris, 25 avril 1984 [n.p.].)

Museum: A resource for learning disabled. New York, The Metropolitan Museum of Art, 1984, 31 pp., illus., bibliogr.
Information for teachers and museum educators who are planning to work with the learning disabled. Summarizes the results of projects developed by the Metropolitan Museum of Art for children with learning disabilities.

Museums and disabled persons. (*Museum*, Paris, UNESCO, Vol. 33, No. 3, 1981, pp. 125–95, illus.)
A special issue brought out in 1981 to mark the 'International Year of Disabled Persons'. It contains a series of articles describing the different initiatives taken in various parts of the world for sufferers from disabilities of whatever kind. It also contains the Declaration of the Rights of the Disabled.

Museums and Handicapped Students: Guidelines for educators. Washington, Smithsonian Institution, 1977, xii, 163 pp., illus., bibliogr.
Publication which, in 1975, recognized the need to develop museum programmes for the handicapped. Survey of museum programmes for handicapped students in the USA, of special education teachers, and guidelines for designing programmes for physically and emotionally handicapped students.

Museums and the Disabled. New York, Metropolitan Museum of Art, 1979, 44 pp., illus., bibliogr.
Basic manual used for the training of volunteers working in the Metropolitan Museum of Art on the integration of disabled visitors with the visiting public. Communication methods used with deaf museum visitors, mentally retarded adults and visually handicapped are described.

Museums and the Handicapped. Seminar organized by the Group for Educational

Select bibliography

Services in Museums, Department of Museum Studies and Adult Education, University of Leicester. Leicester, Leicestershire Museums, Art Galleries and Records Service, 1976, 68 pp., illus., bibliogr.
    A definition of several different handicaps followed by a description of what museums can offer the handicapped through various programmes: provides examples from UK museums (Leicester, Gloucester, Aberdeen, etc.) as well as the Nordic Museum in Sweden and museums in South Africa.

The museums and the handicapped. (In *Music and the museum* (Material concerning the CECA Conference, Warszawa-Torun-Poznan, 1975) ed. by Dominika Cicha. Poznan, Warszawa, Polish National Committee of ICOM, 1976, pp. 108–22, bibliogr.)

Nigam, M. L., On reaching the community: Salar Jung Museum, Hyderabad. (*Museum*, Paris, UNESCO, No. 155, 1987, pp. 139–44, illus.)

1981: Année internationale des personnes handicapées. (*Travées, bulletin des centres culturels de rencontre*, Paris, No. 8, déc. 1981–avr. 1982, p. 9, illus.)

1989 European awards on independent living for disabled people. Helios programme. 1989 [n.p.].
    Folder containing information on the competitors, divided into three categories: A. Mobility and transportation; B. Buildings used by people; C. Housing and supporting services.

Ninko, K. C., Special programmes for special persons: the handicapped. (In *Museum and Tourism. Proceedings of All India Museums Conference*, Bhubaneswar, 1985. New Delhi, Museums Association of India, 1985, pp. 43–7.)

Palmer, Cheryl P., Accessibility for all. (*SEMC Journal*, Charlotte, March 1979, pp. 9–14, bibliogr.)

Paris: musées, bibliothèques, centres et ateliers culturels ... premier guide à l'usage des personnes handicapées à Paris. Paris, Fondation de France and the CNFLRH, 1989, 242 pp.

Park, David C., Ross, Wendy M. and Ellis, W. Kay, *Interpretation for Disabled Visitors in the National Park System.* Washington, National Park Service, 1986, 107 pp., illus.
    Programme accessibility for disabled persons in national parks. Presents a variety of specially designed programmes aimed at full participation and fulfilling experiences. Also gives guidelines for the organization of interpretive services adapted to visually impaired, deaf and mentally retarded visitors.

Pasqualini, N., *Creare a misura dell'ultimo. Legislazione, commenti, esperienze per una città senza barriere.* Legnago: analisi di un centro cittadino. Tesi Laurea univ. Bologna, Fac. Lettere/DAMS, 1985 [n.p.].

Pearson, Anne, Arts for Everyone. Guidance on provision for disabled people. London, Carnegie United Kingdom Trust and Centre on Environment for the Handicapped, 1987, vi, 110 pp., illus.
    After recommendations to help disabled people – what to do and what not to do – Part 2 deals with access, security, adapted furniture, volunteers etc. (Section 2 dealing specifically with museums). Part 3 is devoted to technical design information and Part 4 lists relevant legislation and regulations.

Pearson, Anne, The vicious circle. Museum education and handicapped people in some London museums. (*Journal of Education in Museums*, York, No. 3, 1982, pp. 5–7, illus.)

Report of Activities, 1980–1981. (*Tribune libre*, ICOM International Committee for Public Relations, Mäntta Finland, No. 2, 1981.)
    This issue includes: Programming for persons with handicaps (p. 25); Programme for the blind in the National Museum of Ethnology at Leiden, by Harald S. van der Straaten (p. 47); Induction loop for the hard of learning, by Corinne Bellow (p. 57).

Schleussner, Bernhard, UN-Programm für Behinderte betrifft auch die Museen. (*Museumskunde*, Bonn, Vol. 49, No. 1, 1984, pp. 53–4, illus.)

Snider, Harold, The inviting air of an accessible space. (*Museum News*, Washington, Vol. 55, No. 3, 1977, pp. 18–20, illus.)

Steiner, Charles K., The disabled and works of art. [Paper presented at the Bellagio Seminar,

1984, organized by HAY and Rockefeller Foundation, 1984, 12 pp.]

Steiner, Charles K., German, Amy and Brolley, Wolfgang, Helping learning disabled visitors at the Metropolitan Museum of Art. (*Their World*, New York, Foundation for Children With Learning Disabilities, 1983, pp. 76–7, illus.)

Terry, Paula, New rules will require even greater access to museums. (*Museum News*, Washington, Vol. 69, No. 1, Jan.–Feb. 1990, pp. 26–8.)

Testu, Jean-Michel, Les Activités ordinaires de culture, de sport et de loisirs, bilan et propositions pour la participation des jeunes handicapés. Rapport à Monsieur le Premier Ministre et au Ministre délégué à la jeunesse et aux sports. Paris, 1985, 103 pp.

This Way Please: For easier access to the arts, helping clients with disability. Edinburgh, Artlink and Scottish Arts Council, 1989, 4 pp.
  Booklet describing a video produced and sold by Artlink. This video production, featuring the comedian Ronnie Corbett, highlights the problems experienced by disabled people while visiting art venues.

The Use of Museums by Disabled People. CEH Seminar. Some practical considerations. London, Centre for Environment for the Handicapped, Royal National Institute for the Blind, 1980.

Volontari Associati per i Musei Italiani (VAMI), Conferenza internazionale/ International Conference, Prato, Museo de Arte Contemporanea Luigi Pecci, 26, 27, 28 Maggio 1989. Il ruolo dei volontari dei beni culturali: Museo per la scuola, l'handicap, l'ospedale/The role of volunteers in cultural heritage: Museum for school, handicap, hospital.
  Programme of an international conference organized in 1989.

Working with special groups. (In *Creative museum methods and educational techniques*, by Jeanette Hauck Booth, Gerald Krockover and Paula R. Woods. Springfield, Charles C. Thomas, 1982, pp. 104–18.)

II Funding possibilities

The Adapt Fund: guidelines. (In *Adapt: Access for disabled people to arts premises today*, Dunfermline, Carnegie United Kingdom Trust, 12 March 1990 [5] pp.)
  The Carnegie UK Trust has launched a funding campaign aimed at improving accessibility to museums and other arts venues for disabled persons. The programme called 'Adapt' hopes to raise £1 million through donations, grants and awards schemes.

III Museums and physical disabilities

Access in Denmark: A tourist guide for the disabled. 3rd edn [s.l.], Danish Tourist Board with the Committee for Housing, Nov. 1986, 119 pp. [Museum and sight pp. 71–115.]

Architectural facilities for the disabled. The Hague, The Netherlands Society for Rehabilitation, 1973, 32 pp., illus.

The Arts and 504. A 504 handbook for accessible arts programming. Raleigh, N. Carolina, Barrier-free Environment [for] the National Endowment for the Arts, 1985, 97 pp., illus.
  Publication to help the arts administrator solve the architectural accessibility problems he encounters in his work: practical solutions and approaches to such problems are presented.

Ashby, Helen, York 'Please Touch' Workshop. (*Museums Journal*, London, Vol. 89, No. 8, Nov. 1989, p. 11.)

Azario, Brenda, Accès et parcours pour handicapés en fauteuils de quelques musées de Paris. Paris, Feb. 1971 [note of 4 p.].

Bendiner, R., Tours on wheels. (*Workman and Temple Homestead* [s.l.], Vol. 3, No. 2, Summer 1987.)

Courbeyre, Jean, Le Louvre en fauteuil roulant. (*Faire face*, Paris, Sept. 1989, pp. 17–19, illus.)

Ecole, Huguette, En fauteuil à la découverte du musée d'Orsay. (*Au fil des jours*, Paris, No. 117, 1989, pp. 32–4.)

Select bibliography

Enquête sur l'accessibilité des musées, en particulier pour les handicapés physiques [s.l.], Association des musées de Belgique, Feb. 1971, 17 pp.

Galjaard, Johan, Accessibilité des bâtiments publics aux handicapés. Sous la responsabilité du Conseil néerlandais des Handicapés [s.l.], Oct. 1986, 114 pp., illus. [Chapter V museums].

Gall, Günter, Die Behinderten – ihre Ansprüche an den Museumsbau. (*Museumskunde*, Frankfurt a.M., Vol. 47, No. 2, 1982, pp. 67–71.)

Le Grand Louvre accessible. (*Travail social actualité*, Paris, No. 282, 29 Sept. 1989, p. 15.)

Grandjean, Gilles, Accessibilité des musées nationaux aux personnes handicapées. Paris, Ministère de la Culture et de la Communication, Direction des Musées de France, Service de la muséologie et de l'action culturelle, 1986 [n.p.].

Grosbois, Louis-Pierre, *Handicap physique et construction*. Paris, Edns du Moniteur, Ministère de l'urbanisme et du logement, 1989, 264 pp., illus. [chapter 4.2.5.: 'les musées, expositions et bibliothèques' pp. 205–17].

Grosbois, Louis-Pierre and Araneda, A., *Critères d'accessibilité aux présentations*. Paris, Musée national des sciences et de l'industrie, 1982, 42 pp.

Guía de Madrid para disminudos físicos. Madrid, Cruz Roja Española y Coordinadora Provincial de Minusválidos Físicos, 1980 [n.p.].

Guía urbana de Barcelona para disminudos físicos–Ajuntament de Barcelona. Barcelona, Delegació de Cultura, Servei de publications, 1977 [n.p.].

Howroyd, Lawrence, Access for the disabled. (*Kalori*, Sydney, No. 59–60, 1982, pp. 68–70.)

Kenney, Alice P., *Access to the Past. Museum programs and handicapped visitors. A guide to Section 504, making existing programs and facilities accessible to disabled persons*, Nashville, American Association for State and Local History, 1980, x, 131 pp., illus.
    A historian and an educator developed a special interest in improving the accessibility to historic sites after several years of doing research in museums from a wheelchair.

Results of a survey by questionnaires sent to 750 organizations in the USA and Canada. It underlines the need for museums to publicize their special programmes for handicapped more widely and to recognize that disabled persons have a part to play in local historical organizations.

Kenney, Alice P., Museums from a wheelchair. (*Museum News*, Washington, Vol. 53, No. 4, 1974, pp. 14–17, illus.)

Levin, Michael E., A Picasso show for people in wheelchairs. (*The New York Times*, New York, 5 June 1980.)

Locaux recevant du public: accueil des personnes à mobilité réduite: aspects techniques. Paris, APF [Association des Paralysés de France], Nov. 1988 [n. p.], illus.
    Booklet dealing with laws and regulations controlling exterior and interior circulation, accessibility, toilets and various installations.

Niblett, Kathy, Action for access. (*Museums Journal*, London, Vol. 89, No. 5, Aug. 1989, p. 11.)
    Short list of all the facilities and actions made for disabled people since January 1988 (in a regular column of *Museums Journal* covering museums and disabilities).

Note d'information du Ministère de la Culture. Paris, Direction des Musées de France, Bureau des Relations extérieures, mai 1982 [n.p.].

Orofino, Enrico, *Barriere architettoniche*. Torino, edn Omega, 1980 [n.p.].
    Access guide to Italian public buildings and museums, giving the meeting points, toilets and necessary guides.

Ray, Dilip Kumar, *Museum and Physically Handicapped in India*. Calcutta, Naya Prokash, 1984, 83 pp., bibliogr.

Richard, Anne, *Able to Attend: A good practice guide on access to events for disabled people*. London, NCVO Employment Unit, 1987, 30 pp.

Saint-Martin, Philippe, Accessibilité des lieux culturels. (*Réadaptation*, Paris, No. 338, March 1987, pp. 16–20, illus.) [Special issue: Sport, loisirs et culture des handicapés. ONISEP/CNIR.]

Six fauteuils pour les visiteurs. (*L'Alsace*, 10 May 1988.)

Smithsonian: A guide for disabled visitors. Washington, Smithsonian Institution [1989], 27 pp.

Stuart-Smith, John D., Standards for access by the disabled. (*Kalori*, Sydney, No. 59–60, 1982, pp. 65–8.)

Westerlund, Stella and Knuthammar, Thomas, Handicaps prohibited – travelling exhibitions in Sweden. (*Museum*, Paris, UNESCO, Vol. 33, No. 3, 1981, pp. 176–9, illus.)

Wiener Sehenswürdigkeiten mit dem Rollstuhl erlebt. (*Mobil*, Wien, Aug. 1989 [6 pp.], illus.)

IV Museums and people with impaired vision

Alphen, Jan van, Along the Tigris and the Euphrates. (*The International Journal of Museum Management and Curatorship*, Guildford, Vol. 4, No. 3, 1985, pp. 295–6, illus.)

Alphen, Jan van, Handling a cathedral. (*The International Journal of Museum Management and Curatorship*, Guildford, Vol. 1, No. 4, 1982, pp. 347–56, illus.)

Alphen, Jan van, Tentoonstelling voor visueel gehandicapten in het Museum voor Blinden 1979–1980: De Figur van Boedha. (*Bulletin van de KMKG*, Brussels, No. 52, 1980–1, pp. 223–5.)

Anders Gerien. Ostende, Loost Demuynck, Museum of Modern Art, 1987 [catalogue].

Andersen, Christian, *The Museum and the Disabled.* Elverum, Norsk Skogbruksmuseum, 1981, 12 pp.

Art Horizons, 1990: Report of European Blind Union Conference on Appreciation of Art and Cultural Heritage. Glasgow, Royal National Institute for the Blind and EBU Commission on Cultural Affairs, from 29 to 31 August 1990 [publication will be published in 1991 and will include the 'Liverpool Statement'].

Art museums and the visually handicapped consumer: some issues in approach and design. (*Journal of Visual Impairment and Blindness*, London, Vol. 77, No. 7, Sept. 1983, pp. 330–3.)

Art of the eye: an exhibition on vision. Saint-Paul, Forecast and Minnesota Museum of Art and MSB, from 25 January to 30 March 1986 [catalogue].

Arte da toccare. (*Il polso*, Milan, April 1987, pp. 93–100, illus.)

Eine Ausstellung für Blinde und Sehende. Staatliche Museen zu Berlin, Museumspädagogik, 1983 [n.p.] [exhibition leaflet].

L'aveugle et le musée. (*La lettre d'information*, Paris, Ministère de la Culture, de la Communication, des Grands Travaux et de Bicentenaire, No. 255, 13 Feb. 1989, p. 6.)

'L'aveugle et le musée'. Paris, Direction des Musées de France et Association Valentin Haüy pour le bien des aveugles, 1988, 8 pp., illus. [press file].

Balls for meditation, an exhibition co-produced by 'Atelier des Enfants' of the 'Centre G. Pompidou' and TOM Gallery of Touch Me Art, from 5 Sept. to 9 Sept. 1988, 16th World Congress of Rehabilitation International, 15 Oct. to 27 Nov. 1988, Tokyo.

Bartijn, Nicole and Grundmann, Anca, Musea en visueel gehandicapten: het toegankelijk maken van (museale) aktiviteiten voor blinde en slechtziende mensen. Leiden, Feb. 1990 [n.p.] [thesis submitted to the Reinwardt Academie (Faculteit museologie van de Amsterdamse Hogeschool voor de Kunsten)].

Bateman, Penny, 'Human Touch' British Museum exhibition 6 Feb. to 16 March 1986, comments and ideas. (*British Journal of Visual Impairment*, London, No. 4, Summer 1986, pp. 77–9.)

Bedekar, V.H., Display techniques according to some special categories of visitors. (*Studies in Museology*, Baroda, University of Baroda, Department of Museology, No. 13–14, 1979, pp. 70–4.)

Behling, Silke, Tastausstellungen und museumspädagogische Recherchen für Blinde und Sehbehinderte in Marl und Neuss am 11 und 12 Juli 1989. Hannover, Sprengel Museum Hannover, 1989 [unpublished manuscript].

Benke, Uwe, Besuch in einem ungewöhnlichen

Select bibliography

Museum. Das Museum für Blindenwesen in Berlin. (*Kriegsblinden Jahrbuch* [s.l.], 1989, pp. 29–33.)

Bergman, Thomas, Unsere Finger sehen: Blinde Kinder erzählen. Luzern, 1987 (2nd edn).

Boucher, Louise, Les services pour handicapés visuels dans les musées; examen de la situation et des méthodes d'application. Montréal, Département d'anthropologie, Faculté des Arts et Sciences, Université de Montréal, Dec. 1982, 107 pp., annexes, bibliogr. [Ph.D. thesis].
> The author starts by giving a definition of blindness. She then examines the role of museums for the visually handicapped and gives an international overview of cultural policies and of initiatives taken in Canada. There follows a study of the different methods put into practice and of the prospects in Quebec.

Bourgeois-Lechartier, Michel, Friendship: the most powerful force. (*Museum*, Paris, UNESCO, Vol. 33, No. 3, 1981, pp. 160–5, illus.)

Bowden, D.H., Special exhibition for the benefit of blind persons arranged in the Natal Museum. (*SAMAB* [*South African Museums Association Bulletin*], Cape Town, Vol. 8, No. 11, Dec. 1966.)

Bronsdon Rowan, Madeline and Rogow, Sally, Making museums meaningful for blind children. (*Gazette*, Ottawa, Vol. 11, No. 3, 1978, pp. 36–41.)

Calhoun, Sally N., On the edge of vision. (*Museum News*, Washington, Vol. 52, No. 7, 1974, pp. 36–41.)

Cronk, Michael Sam, Blindness and the museum experience. (*Ontario Museum Quarterly*, Toronto, Vol. 12, No. 3, Sept. 1983, pp. 13–15, illus.)

Dalton, Fay, The tactile mobile museum: its history and development. (*Environment Southwest*, San Diego, No. 444, May 1972, pp. 4–5, illus.)

Destrée-Heymans, Thérèse, A la découverte de la sculpture. (*Bulletin des Musées Royaux d'Art et d'Histoire*, Bruxelles, 1971–2, pp. 215–18.)

Directory of Museums with Facilities for Visually Handicapped People. London, Royal National Institute for the Blind, 1988, 31 pp.
> This publication lists 50 places of interest in the UK, mostly museums, which encourage tactile discovery.

Donadoni, Anna, Touching art: the museum of Egyptian antiquities in Turin and the blind. (*A Future for our Past*, Strasbourg, Council of Europe, No. 31, 1987, p. 16.)
> The problem of damage to works of art is now solved, the article deals with the initiation of blind people into the practice of museum-visiting via braille data sheets and relief drawings.

Duchateau, Sylvie, L'accès des aveugles aux musées et expositions ... du changement! J'ai visité le château de Blois. (*Comme les autres*, Paris, No. 97, 1988.)

Duczmal-Pacowska, Halina, The museum and the blind. (*Museum*, Paris, UNESCO, Vol. 28, No. 3, 1976, pp. 172–4.)

Egger, Michael and Knorr, Michael, Blindenführung in der prähistorishen Staatssammlung München. (*Museumskunde*, Frankfurt a.M., Vol. 45, No. 2, 1980, p. 77.)

Enzmann, Christel and Germer, Ernest, Eine Sonderausstellung für Blinde im Museum für Völkerkunde zu Leipzig. (*Neue Museumskunde*, Berlin, Vol. 4, No. 4, 1971, pp. 288–93.)

Um Estudo sobre a equivalencia entre a percepçao visual e a percepçao tactil. Rio de Janeiro, 1968.

Favière, Jean, Duczmal, Halina and Delevoy-Otlet, S., The museum and the blind. (*Museum*, Paris, UNESCO, Vol. 28, No. 3, 1976, pp. 172–6, illus.)

Feeling your way through Rodin? (*The Japan Times Weekly* [Tokyo], 8 Sept. 1984, p. 4.)

Fiedeler-Sennett, Corinna, Recherchen über das Blindenmuseum Berlin im Museum für Völkerkunde. Hannover, Sprengel Museum Hannover, 1989 [unpublished manuscript].

Ford Smith, James, A sense of touch. (*Museums Journal*, London, Vol. 83, No. 2–3, 1983, p. 143.)

Fromhagen, Ute-Brigitta, Mit den Händen sehen: Skulpturen verhelfen blinden Menschen zum Kunsterlebnis. (*Kunst und Antiquitäten*, Frankfurt, No. 5, 1980, pp. 87–92.)

Galipeau-Dore, Mireille, Expériences d'animation auprès des handicapés visuels. (*Muséo-vision*, Montréal, Vol. 4, No. 1–2, 1980, p. 24.)

Giraudy, Danièle and Thevenin, Marie-José, Les mains regardent. Paris, Centre Georges Pompidou, 1977 [n.p.], illus. [exhibition catalogue].
   Third exhibition organized at the Georges Pompidou Centre by 'The children's workshop'. Exhibition details with pictures and articles or book extracts about the blind and their perception.

Goldberg, Joshua, In praise of darkness: the 'Hands-on Japan' exhibition. (*Museum*, Paris, UNESCO, Vol. 33, No. 3, 1981, pp. 187–92, illus.)

Grandjean, Gilles, L'accueil des personnes aveugles et mal-voyantes dans les musées. Paris, Direction des Musées de France, Service de l'Action Culturelle, 1987, 4 pp.

Groff, Gerda and Garner, Laura, What museum guides need to know: access for blind and visually impaired visitors. New York, American Foundation for the Blind, 1989, 55 pp., illus.
   Presents problems specific to the blind and how to behave with them. Gives advice on facilitating access and on organizing activities, special programmes and tactile exhibitions.

Hansson, Anna, Working with blind people at Nordiska Museet and Skansen. (*Market of Ideas*, Stockholm, Nordiska Museet [for] ICOM–CECA, No. 9, 1976, pp. 3–5.)

Haseltine, James L., Please touch. (*Museum News*, Washington, Vol. 45, No. 2, 1966, pp. 11–16, illus.)

Henriksen, Harry C., Your museum: a resource for the blind. (*Museum News*, Washington, Vol. 50, No. 2, 1971, pp. 26–8, illus.)

Jones, Rachel and Jones, Lewis, Beauty by touch. (*New Beacon*, London, RNIB, Nov. 1988, p. 348.)

Junginger, Gabriele, Museumspädagogische Angebote für Blinde Besucher – eine Bestandsaufnahme. (*Sonderpädagogik* [s.l.], No. 3, July 1989, pp. 118–22.)

Kefakis, Emmanuel, 'Tactual Museum'. Lighthouse for the Blind. Athens, Greece. Athens, 1988, 5 pp. [Paper presented at the EMYA Seminar, Delphi, May 1988.]

Kirby, William, Engaging the imagination. (*Artists Newsletters*, Sunderland, Jan. 1990, p. 20 [Report on international conference 'Art Education and Visual Impairment', Liverpool, Tate Gallery, May 1989].)

Klein, Heijo, Blindenführungen in Kölner Museen. (In *Die Praxis der Museumsdidaktik. Bericht über ein internationales Seminar der deutschen Unesco-Kommission, veranstaltet in Zusammenarbeit mit dem Museum Folkwang vom 23. bis 26. Nov. 1971, in Essen.* Pullach/München, Verlag Dokumentation for Deutsche UNESCO-Kommission, 1974, pp. 65–9.)

Kobbert, Max J., Bilder für Blinde und Sehende. (*Horus* [s.l.], Vol. 40, No. 1, 1978, p. 2.)

Kolar, Judith Rena, A bird in the hand: planning a zoo program for the blind. (*Curator*, New York, Vol. 24, No. 2, 1981, pp. 97–108, illus.)

Kriedler, Richard, Blinde im Museum.(*Museen in Köln*, Köln, Vol. 11, No. 2, Feb. 1972, pp. 1022–3, illus.)

Lange, Margarete, *Diareihe zur ästhetischen Erziehung. Strandortbestimmung und Neuorientierung, Kongressbericht.* XXIX Kongress für Sehgeschädigtenpädagogik, Würzburg, 1–5 Aug. 1983, pp. 140–1.

Lauritzen, Eva Maehre, *Museums and the Handicapped: Adapting the museum for the blind and weak sighted.* Oslo, Association of Norwegian Museum Educators, 1985, 18 pp., illus.
   Conclusions of a seminar organized by the Norwegian Museum Educators Association in 1981. Short report in the form of a 'checklist' of measures to be taken by museums to enable them to receive physically disabled visitors, including building requirements, exhibition principles, quality and readability

of texts, use of models, guided tours, special personnel trained as 'escorts' for blind persons.

Levi, Fabio, Toccare l'arte. (*Rassegna stampa handicap* [Torino], 8–9 Feb. 1986, pp. 24–7, illus.)

Liblin, Lawrence, To touch and to hear. (*ICOM Education*, Paris, ICOM–CECA, No. 7, 1975–6, pp. 36–7, illus.)

Liebelt, Udo (ed.), Museum der Sinne. Hannover, Sprengel Museum, 1990, 142 pp. illus. (Museums Pädagogik.)

Liebelt, Udo, Skulptur begreifen: Tastgalerie für Sehende und Blinde im Kunstmuseum Hannover mit Sammlung Sprengel. (*Kunst und Therapie*, Münster, No. 3, 1983, pp. 100–5.)

Madinier, Claire. Quand les mains regardent. (*La Croix*, Paris, 24 May 1982 [n.p.].)

Maquette d'exploration architecturale pour les non-voyants. (*L'Ami des musées*, Paris, No. 2, Nov. 1988, p. 44, illus.)

Materials from the National Arts and the Handicapped Information Service. Washington, April 1978, 24 pp.
File comprising numerous articles, among which: Museums and the blind, by Harold Snider (pp. 7–11); Exhibitions for visually impaired, by Maya Reid (pp. 12–14); A gallery of the senses, by Pat Mulcahy (pp. 14–17); From the inner eye, by Edgar Nice (pp. 19–21).

Moore, George, Displays for the sightless. (*Curator*, New York, Vol. 11, No. 4, 1968, pp. 292–6.)

The museum and the visually impaired. The report of the Work Group on facilities for the visually impaired. Toronto, Royal Ontario Museum, 1980, 23 pp.

Nair, S. N., Special programmes for blind children at the National Museum of Natural History, New Delhi. (*Museum*, Paris, UNESCO, Vol. 33, No. 3, 1981, pp. 174–5, illus.)

Naito, Hiroshi, Gallery of touch-me art. (*The Japan architect* [Tokyo], No. 330, 1984, pp. 26–31.)

Objekte zum Anlassen, Museum für Kunst und Gewerbe. Hamburg, 1981 [n.p.]. [Katalog von C. Enghausen.]

Olsen, Marion, A touch sight exhibit. (*Lore*, Milwaukee, Vol. 25, No. 3, 1975, pp. 20–3, illus.)

Othman, Erica and Levanto, Marjetta, Pictures for listening. (*Ateneum Taidemuseo*, Helsinki, Vol. 29, 1987 [n.p.].)

Ouvrir le musée aux aveugles. (*Le Valentin Haüy*, Paris, Association Valentin Haüy pour le bien des aveugles, No. 16, 1989, pp. 10–11.)
A competition organized by the Valentin Haüy Association for the blind which invites museum curators to draw up a museographical project for blind visitors.

Pearson, Anne, Please touch. An exhibition of animal sculpture at the British Museum. (*The International Journal of Museum Management and Curatorship*, Guildford, Vol. 3, No. 4, 1984, pp. 373–8, illus.)

Pearson, Fiona, Sculpture for the blind: National Museum of Wales. (*Museums Journal*, London, Vol. 81, No. 1, 1981, pp. 35–7, illus.)

Plastik zum Begreifen: Kunstausstellung für Blinde und Sehende. (*Augenoptik*, Berlin (Ost), Vol. 101, No. 5, 1984, pp. 152–3.)

Raemdonck, M. van, Museum voor Blinden. (*Museumleven*, Brugge, No. 5, 1978, pp. 27–30.)

Raemdonck, M. van and Homes-Fredericq, D., Lang Tigris en Eufraat. (*Bulletin van de K.M.K.G.*, Brussels, 56/1, 1985, pp. 154–6.)

Raffray, Monique, The arts through touch perception: present trends and future prospects. (*The British Journal of Visual Impairment*, London, Vol. 6, No. 2, Summer 1988, pp. 63–5.)

Reading Images by Touch or Vision. [Seminar] Brussels, 23 Sept. 1989 [proceedings in preparation].

Rowland, William, Museums and the blind: It feels like a flower … (*ICOM News*, Paris, Vol. 26, No. 3, 1973, pp. 117–21, illus.)

Ruyssinck, Micheline, Animal symbole, Animal sacré. (*Bulletin des Musées Royaux d'Art et d'Histoire*, Brussels, tome 57, 1986, p. 159.)

Ruyssinck, Micheline, Les aveugles dans les musées. Bruxelles, mai 1982 [n.p.] [conférence].

Ruyssinck, Micheline, Le musée pour aveugle au Musée Royaux d'Art et d'Histoire 1970–1989: vingt années d'activités. (*Bulletin des Musées Royaux d'Art et d'Histoire*, Bruxelles, No. 60, 1990.)

Saley, Mahamane, Action to help the blind and physically handicapped, Niger National Museum, Niamey. (*Museum*, Paris, UNESCO, Vol. 28, No. 4, 1976, pp. 210–11, illus.)

Scherf-Smith, Patricia, Against segregating the blind. (*Museum News*, Washington, Vol. 55, No. 3, Jan./Feb. 1977, pp. 10–11.)

Schütte, Christiane, Durch Blinde sehen gelernt. (*Jahrbuch für Blindenfreunde* [s.l.], 1980, 25 pp.)

Service de visites guidées pour non/mal-voyants au Musée du Duomo de Milan. VAMI [Volontari Associati per Musei Italiani]. [Milano, 1989, note of 5 pp.]
A short definition of the Italian Association of Museum Volunteers (VAMI) is followed by a description of the methods developed by the group 'Museums and Handicapped' which, after a study of the psychological reactions of the blind, has prepared didactic texts in braille, as part of a programme devised by a psychologist and a blind teacher at the Institute for the Blind. A detailed report of a museum visit by a group of young blind people completes this help programme for volunteers.

Shore, Irma and Jacinto, Beatrice, *Access to Art: A museum directory for blind and visually impaired people*. New York, American Foundation for the Blind and Museum of American Folk Art, 1989, xiv, 129 pp., bibliogr.

Skulptur begreifen. Tastgalerie. Kunstmuseum Hannover mit Sammlung Sprengel. Hannover, 1989 [catalogue].

Smith, Sheila, The spirit of the material. (*New Beacon*, London, RNIB, April 1988, pp. 114–17, illus.)

Sofka, Vinos, Stereo copying: a new means of communicating with the visually disabled.

(*MuWoP/Museological Working Papers*, Paris, ICOM, No. 2, 1981, pp. 81–2.)

[Special issue on museums and disabled people] (*Museum News: The Journal of National Heritage, The Museums Action Movement*, London, ed. Camilla Boodle, No. 45, Autumn 1989, 8 pp.)

Spitzer, Klaus, *Bildnerische Gestaltung und Kunstbetrachtung in der Blindenpädagogik. Standortbestimmung und Neuorientierung. Kongressbericht*. XXIX Kongress für Sehgeschädigtenpädagogik, Würzburg, 1–5 Aug., 1983, pp. 136–9.)

Spitzer, Klaus, Blinde im Museum. (*Tasten und Gestalten*, Waldkirch, 1982, p. 398.)

Stanford, Charles W., The Mary Duke Biddle Gallery for the Blind. (*ICOM Annual, Museum, Education, Cultural Action*, Paris, No. 1, 1969, pp. 23–4.)

Stanford, Charles W., A museum gallery for the blind. (*Museum News*, Washington, Vol. 44, No. 10, 1966, pp. 18–23, illus.)

Steinke, Gioya, Beauty by touch. (*New Beacon*, London, RNIB, Sept. 1989, p. 326 [text on exhibition 'Art at Heart', London, from 3 Oct. to 14 Dec. 1989].)

Steinke, Gioya, Time to focus. (*Artists Newsletter*, Sunderland, Jan. 1990, p. 21.)

Sturm, Lotte, Blinde begreifen Kunst. (*Kunstpädagogik* [s.l.], No. 2, 1979, pp. 20–2.)

Sturm, Lotte, Gegen das Berührungstabu in den Museen. (*Jahrbuch für Blindenfreunde* [s.l.], 1980, p. 17.)

Sturm, Lotte, Kunstbetastungen. (*Museumskunde*, Frankfurt a.M., Vol. 45, No. 2, 1980, pp. 72–6, illus.)

Sturm, Lotte, Sonderschule und Museum. (*Zeitung der Schule für Geistigbehinderte des Kreises Kaarst Holzbüttgen*, Neuss, No. 2, 1987.)

The Tactual Museum of Athens: an educational resource for the blind. (*Museum*, Paris, UNESCO, No. 162, 1989, pp. 78–9.)
Interview with Mrs Iphigenia Polydorou-Benaki about the Museum for the Blind in Athens which exhibits plaster copies of statues, vases, bas relief.

Select bibliography

Talking touch. Report on a seminar on the use of touch in museums and galleries held at the RNIB on 29th February 1988. Jointly organized with MAGDA (Museums and Galleries Disability Association). London, Royal National Institute for the Blind, 1988, 50 pp.
> Papers delivered at the 'Talking touch' seminar. Contributions from various museum curators and researchers in the field of tactile art are given, as well as a useful list of organizations working in this field.

Tissu tact 1989: Trois musées, une exposition itinérante accessible aux non et mal-voyants. Musée archéologique départemental du Val d'Oise, Musées d'Aurillac, Musée Denon de Châlon-sur-Saône. Conseil général du Val d'Oise avec le concours de la Fondation de France, 1989 [n. p.], illus. [press file].

Tourolle, Martine, Culture et handicaps: L'expression d'autres sensibilités: le rêve au bout des doigts. (*Revue de la mutualité*, Paris, No. 114, Dec. 1983, pp. 26–7.)

Townsend, Sally, Touch and see – architecture for the blind. (*Curator*, New York, Vol. 18, No. 3, 1975, pp. 200–5.)

Turner, Ailsa, An eye for art. (*New Beacon*, London, RNIB, Nov. 1988, p. 346 [Report on the exhibition of work by visually impaired artists held at Gunnersbury Park Museum in Oct. 1988].)

Vanbelle, François, Une approche tactile de la sculpture par les non voyants est-elle possible? (*Bulletin pédagogique*, Paris, No. 108, 1987, pp. 7–13.)

Vanbelle, François, L'exposition 'Visages de l'homme'. Une première au Musée d'art et d'essai à Paris. (*Musées et collections publiques de France*, Paris, Vol. 162, No. 1, 1984, pp. 29–34.)

Vanbelle, François, Musées pour aveugles dans le monde: quelques aspects de participation des aveugles à la vie des musées et plus particulièrement des musées d'arts plastiques dans les domaines de la sculpture et des arts décoratifs. (*La revue d'esthétique*, Paris, No. 2, 1971, pp. 185–96.)

Voigt, Elisabeth, The extra-mural museum. (*SAMAB* [*South African Museums Association Bulletin*], Cape Town, Vol. 10, No. 4, Dec. 1972, pp. 162–9.)

Vorreiter, Gabrielle, The stage of touch. (*Architectural Review*, London, June 1989 [n.p.].)

Wasala, Blanka, Wielka przygoda klasy IV (refleksje nauczycielki Szkoly Podstawowej dla Dzieci Niewidomych W Laskach). [Une grande aventure de la 4ème classe. Des réflexions de l'institutrice de l'école primaire pour les enfants aveugles à Laski.] Warszawa, Osrodek dokumentacji zabyków, 1984, pp. 70–6, illus.

Watkins, Malcolm J., A small handling table for blind visitors. (*Museums Journal*, London, Vol. 75, No. 1, 1975, pp. 29–30.)

Weisen, Marcus, Art in touch. (*Artists Newsletter*, Sunderland, Dec. 1988, pp. 29–31, illus.)
> The author outlines the value of tactile sense. Do touch exhibitions have an aesthetic of their own or are they simply another form of contact with art?

Weisen, Marcus, Art to share. Art at heart. (*New Beacon*, London, RNIB, Sept. 1989, pp. 320–4 [text on exhibition 'Art at Heart', London, from 3 Oct. to 14 Dec. 1989].)

Weisen, Marcus, Cultural integration and creativity of visually handicapped people: towards a European policy. (*New Beacon*, London, RNIB, Feb. 1988, pp. 47–9, March 1988, pp. 83–5.)

Weisen, Marcus, Museums and the visually impaired visitor. (*Museums Journal*, London, Vol. 89, No. 7, Oct. 1989, p. 11.)

Weisen, Marcus and Hammond, David, Gateway, proposal for a tactile museum of environmental discovery. London, Royal National Institute for the Blind, 1987, ix, 95 pp., 7 appendices, bibliogr.

Wexell, Astrid, In touch with history. (*Social Design*, Stockholm, 1981 [n.p.].)

Wexell, Astrid, Känn var historia ett läromedel för synskedede Skolbarn. (*Svenska museer*, Stockholm, No. 3, 1980, pp. 27–30.)

Wexell, Astrid, Tactile pictures in Stockholm. (*Museum*, Paris, UNESCO, Vol. 33, No. 3, 1981, pp. 180–3, illus.)

Williams, Sally, Eine Galerie zum Tasten. (*Jahrbuch für Blindenfreunde* [s.l.], 1980, p. 25.)

V Museums and people with impaired hearing

Bizaguet, Eric, Evolution de la prise en charge du déficient auditif dans les musées et spectacles. Paris, Jan. 1989 [note of 7 pp.].
A definition of defective hearing and a list of the factors creating difficulties for those who suffer from it. A review of the various technical aids: the magnetic loop, infra-red system and high-frequency communication, with the merits and drawbacks of each according to circumstances.

Deaf aide guides deaf visitors. (*The Torch*, Washington DC, The Smithsonian Institution, 1980 [n.p.].)

Feeley, Jennifer, The 'listening eye': tours for the deaf in San Francisco Bay Area Museums. (*Museum Studies Journal*, San Francisco, Vol. 2, No. 1, 1985, pp. 36–49, illus.)

Haase, Peter Norreso, Video-museum med muligheder. (*DTM* [*Dansk Tidsskrift for Museumsformidling*], Kobenhavn, No. 7, 1984, pp. 22–7, illus.)

Sign-language Program. New York, The Metropolitan Museum of Art, Division of Education Services, Spring 1989.

Sutherland, Mimi, Total communication [programmes for the deaf]. (*Museum News*, Washington, Vol. 55, No. 3, 1977, pp. 25–6, illus.)

Tennenbaum, Paula, Soundtracks: intern develops new audiences. (*The Museologist*, Rochester, Vol. 46, No. 167, Spring 1984, pp. 8–10, illus.)

Veit, Paul and Bizaguet, Geneviève, La prothèse auditive, ses compléments et ses extensions, évolutions récentes et perspectives d'avenir. (*Réadaptation*, Paris, No. 349, April 1988.)

VI Museums and mentally disabled people

Camargo e Almeida, Fernanda de, Museum of images of the unconscious, Rio de Janeiro. An experience lived within a psychiatric hospital. (*Museum*, Paris, UNESCO, Vol. 28, No. 1, 1976, pp. 34–41, illus.)

Le musée: lieu d'accueil et de rencontres avec les personnes handicapées mentales. Concours. (*Cahiers du Temps libre. Culture, Loisirs, Sports*, Paris, Jan. 1990, 12 pp. [special issue].)
For its 30th birthday, UNAPEI (Union of Associations of Mentally Handicapped Persons, Parents and Friends) organized a competition with the Fondation de France and the Direction des Musées de France. It aims to integrate mentally disabled persons into cultural life, through the discovery of the artistic, technical and scientific heritage. This issue also includes the information circular sent to French museum directors and a list of French museums having reception services for mentally handicapped persons.

Museum Education for Retarded Adults. Reaching out to a neglected audience. New York, Metropolitan Museum of Art, 1979, 47 pp., illus., bibliogr.

Ouertani, Nayla, A new source of hope: a scheme for mentally handicapped children in Tunisia. (*Museum*, Paris, UNESCO, Vol. 33, No. 3, 1981, pp. 172–4, illus.)

Rudge, Maureen, Museums – a therapy for the disabled. (*Kalori*, Sydney, No. 59–60, 1982, pp. 76–8.)

Steiner, Charles, Reaching the mentally handicapped. (*Museum News*, Washington, Vol. 56, No. 6, 1978, pp. 19–24, illus.)

Tourolle, Martine, Culture et handicaps: l'expression d'autres sensibilités. Naïfs, primaires ou géniaux. (*Revue de la mutualité*, Paris, No. 114, Dec. 1983, pp. 34–5.)

Note on the Fondation de France and ICOM

The Fondation de France

The Fondation de France is a private, non-profit-making body created on the initiative of General de Gaulle and André Malraux to help individuals, associations and companies carry out charitable, cultural and scientific projects of general interest. It was founded in 1969 by a group of French public and private financial institutions.

The Fondation de France has a three-fold mission. It collects funds from private individuals and business firms to serve urgent social needs in numerous fields: poverty and social integration, scientific and medical research, promotion of arts and culture, protection and rehabilitation of the environment, help for the Third World and eastern Europe. It offers to any people wanting to carry out charitable works on an individual basis the possibility of creating their own foundation. It promotes the development of associations by providing them with services and advice such as administration of funds, legal recognition, etc.

The Fondation de France is non-denominational and apolitical. It is state independent and governed by private law.
Fondation de France, 40 avenue Hoche, 75008 Paris, France.

ICOM: The International Council of Museums

The International Council of Museums (ICOM) is a non-profit-making organization dedicated to the improvement and advancement of museums and the museum profession. Founded in 1946, it provides a world-wide communications network for museum people of all disciplines and specialities. It counts over 8,000 members in some 120 countries. It is associated with UNESCO as a category 'A' Non-Governmental Organ-ization. Its Paris-based Secretariat and Information Centre assure the day-to-day running of the organization and the co-ordination of its activities and programmes.

ICOM Secretariat and Information Centre, 1 rue Miollis, 75732 Paris Cedex 15, France.

List of contributors

Jan Daniel Artymowski, of the Royal Castle of Warsaw in Poland.

Louis Avan is Professor at CNAM–Laboratoire B. Frybourg in Paris.

Iphigenia Benaki is Assistant Director at the Tactual Museum for the Blind in Kallithea, Greece.

Robert Benoist is President of the Valentin Haüy Association in Paris.

Eric Bizaguet works on hearing aids at the Laboratoire de protection auditive in Paris.

Guy Bouchauveau is Technical attaché at the Cité des Sciences et de l'Industrie de la Villette in Paris.

Michel Bourgeois-Lechartier is Curator – PAICA, Conservation Départementale des Musées in Lons le Saunier.

Nancy Breitenbach is Head of Disabled Persons Programme at the Fondation de France in Paris.

Dominique Charvet is Technical Adviser at the Ministère de la Culture in Paris.

Hoëlle Corvest is Scientific and Technical Attaché at the Cité des Sciences et de l'Industrie de la Villette in Paris.

Piero Cosulich is an architect in Milan, Italy.

Béatrice Derycke is President of the Association Art Visuel International des Sourds in Paris.

Pascal Dubois is the Head of Technical Services, Service National 'Accessibilité', Association des Paralysés de France in Paris.

Alain Erlande-Brandenburg is Assistant Director of the Musées de France, Paris.

Francisco García Aznarez is an engineer at CYP in Madrid, Spain.

Zoltan Gollesz, of the Hadtörteneti Muzeum in Budapest, Hungary.

Gilles Grandjean is Curator at the Musée des Beaux Arts in Rouen, France.

Louis-Pierre Grosbois is an architect in Paris.

William Kirby is a consultant in art and design in Winchester.

Anne Magnant, of the French Directorate of the Heritage, Ministère de la Culture in Paris.

207

List of contributors

Roland May is Curator of the Archaeological Museum – Musée Borely-Château Borely in Marseille, France.

Bernard Mottez is Director of Studies, CEMS at the Ecole des hautes études en sciences sociales in Paris.

Anne Pearson, of the British Museum in London and Secretary of MAGDA, the Museums and Galleries Disabilities Association.

C. C. Pei is an architect with I. M. Pei and Partners, New York.

Jean-Paul Philippon is an architect in Paris.

Jean de Ponthieu is Director of a specialized institution in Chavagnac Lafayette, France.

Janine Prudhomme is Curator of the Musée d'histoire naturelle in Bordeaux, France.

Mieke van Raemdonck, of the Musées Royaux d'art et d'histoire in Brussels, Belgium.

Gert Reising, of the Staatliche Kunsthalle Karlsruhe in Karlsruhe, Germany.

Micheline Ruyssinck, of the Musées Royaux d'art et d'histoire in Brussels, Belgium.

Angelika Schmidt-Herwig, of the Museum Fruehgesschichte in Frankfurt am Main, Germany.

Frans Schouten, formerly of the Reinwardt Academie in Leiden, The Netherlands.

Peter Senior is Director of Arts for Health at Manchester Polytechnic.

Charles K. Steiner, of The Art Museum, Princeton University, New Jersey, USA.

Emese Szoleczky, of Hadtörteneti Muzeum in Budapest, Hungary.

Martine Tissier de Mallerais is Curator of the Musée de Blois in France.

Sylvie Tsyboula is Assistant Director of the Fondation de France in Paris.

Bernhard Wehrens is Director of the Division of Programmes for the Disabled, EC, Brussels, Belgium.

Marcus Weisen is Director of the Royal National Institute for the Blind in London.

Index

Index

210

Index

Index